LECTURELESS

PRAISE FOR *LECTURELESS*

As a former social studies teacher and current college professor, I have found the book I will be using for all of my social studies pedagogy courses. For decades, social studies teachers have fought the stereotype of the boring teacher droning on through lectures followed by reading a textbook and giving a test focused solely on names and dates. Lewer offers a compelling alternative that reminds us of all of the great social studies teachers who break with this stereotype. He shares big ideas of authentic learning with a clear recognition for how this can be accomplished when teaching a significant amount of content in a tested area. He shares multiple models for how we can learn history at a deeper level through relevance and authenticity.

—**Dr. John Spencer,** Associate Professor of Education at George Fox University and author of *Empower: What Happens When Students Own Their Learning*

Dan Lewer reminds us that amazing things happen when a passionate, knowledgeable educator connects research-based instructional practices with the needs of students. This is a wonderful book for new or experienced teachers in the authentic voice of a practicing educator who loves teaching.

—**Bruce Lesh,** author of *Why Won't You Just Tell Us the Answer: Teaching Historical Thinking in Grades 7–12*

I've followed Dan Lewer's work for years, and I've always been inspired by his passion for history education. *Lectureless* reflects the same infectious energy he's famous for. It's also a straightforward, practical guide for teachers looking to move beyond the usual so their classroom can feel relevant and memorable. This is the book I wish existed when I started teaching.

—**Luke Rosa,** founder of Students of History

Schools around the world are all trying to figure out solutions to the same challenges: how to move learners from being passive to active, from disengaged to engaged, and from being receivers of subject material to being thinkers, problem solvers, and agents of their own learning. *Lectureless* paves the way for what this transformation looks like from a history-class perspective. Dan shares his passion for teaching, providing readers with a plethora of lived examples, activities, and structures that all help students appreciate history, love learning, and begin to think like historians. A welcome addition to the field, *Lectureless* is a book I will revisit for years to come.

—**Trevor MacKenzie,** education consultant and author

We already have so many books about history, but what's missing is a book for educators about *how* to teach history at the secondary level. This is the type of expertise that is absent from most general credential programs. I have known Dan for years, and I'm thrilled that he is turning his passion and brilliance into a manual for new and veteran teachers who want to get through to this next generation of learners and civic leaders.

—**Lauren Cella,** history teacher and creator of the series Gen Z Teaches History

Dan's infectious enthusiasm is backed by real, classroom-tested strategies that make history feel urgent and alive. He reminds us that engaging students in critical inquiry isn't just possible; it's essential and can be downright joyful.

—**Glen Coleman,** award winning teacher, author of *Teaching in the New Crazy: On Thriving in an Overwhelming, Politicized, and Complicated World*

DAN LEWER

TEACHING HISTORY TO ENGAGE AND EMPOWER

Lectureless: Teaching History to Engage and Empower

This book is available at special discounts when purchased in quantity for educational purposes or for use as premiums, promotions, or fundraisers. For inquiries and details, contact the publisher at books@daveburgessconsulting.com.

Published by Dave Burgess Consulting, Inc.
Vancouver, WA
DaveBurgessConsulting.com

Library of Congress Control Number: 2026943860
Paperback ISBN: 978-1-968898-23-6
Ebook ISBN: 978-1-968898-24-3

Cover and interior design by Liz Schreiter
Edited and produced by Reading List Editorial
ReadingListEditorial.com

To the teachers who inspired me to
become an educator and to my students
at Honoka'a High and Intermediate
School who made me love being one.

CONTENTS

INTRODUCTION

It was the first day back after summer break. That glorious day when the room is yours—before the staff icebreakers, before the new group of students arrive. A blank canvas on which to paint a new school year.

I was centering my Muhammad Ali poster on the wall when a student and her mom approached. "E-ten. This is going to be your history class, Hope." A nervous freshman scanned the room, looking right past me, and locked onto the stack of textbooks.

"Don't worry." I smiled, crouching to meet her eyes. "We won't be using those much. But we will be doing all sorts of other activities I think you're really going to enjoy."

Her mom gave a cautious laugh. "She's never really liked history."

"I'm just not . . . good at it," Hope quietly clarified.

Never liked history? Isn't good at it? Who has tortured this poor girl? I thought.

"Well," I assured Hope, "I bet you are going to really enjoy learning history this year! And I promise, if you just give it a chance, I'll do my best to make it a fun class where you learn something interesting every day." I held out a pinkie to seal the deal. That cheered her up some, but she soon took off with Mom to continue the campus tour.

Those statements, though—"never really liked history" and "I'm just not *good* at history"—stuck with me. As I set up the bulletin boards, hung up my posters, and chipped the previous year's gum deposits off the bottom of desks, I wondered about it.

What are students thinking of when they say they're not good at or don't like history? Memorizing facts out of context? Enduring lifeless lectures? Filling in blanks from a PowerPoint or trudging through chapter after chapter of a textbook? Storing up facts, memorizing, and depositing them on the unit exam?

By that standard, I'm not very good at history. And I sure as heck wouldn't like it much either.

But history is so much more interesting, meaningful, and important than just memorizing facts about the past. History isn't just about the answers. It's about the questions and the investigation. It's detective work—scrutinizing documents, interrogating evidence, piecing together a story of who we are. It's debating ideas and wrestling with controversy. It's not *just* about how we got here. It's what we do now. History education *is* the training ground for citizenship.

But is that how most students experience the discipline of history? Is that what Hope thought of when she reflected on her time in history class? Despite all the educational reforms to move toward active learning, inquiry, and hands-on engagement, many students are still experiencing history primarily as a sit-and-receive class. Through lecture, worksheets, and textbooks, learners are simply being told the answers to questions they never cared to ask.

Is it any wonder why education is having an engagement and relevancy crisis?

As a new teacher still learning the ropes, I learned a lot reflecting on Hope's comments. She made me realize that we don't actually get a blank canvas to start the school year. Students come in with their experiences, their impressions, and the beliefs they've formed about themselves as learners. Some believe history is too hard and it's not for them. Others come in already checked out. They're convinced history is not just boring—it's irrelevant, useless. Why strive for excellence and put forth the effort needed for rigorous scholarship when you don't see any value in learning history? And if you can just google it or ask ChatGPT, why study it to begin with?

And thus, many disengage. They go through the motions but avoid the serious, focused struggle that makes the study of history, *or anything*, worthwhile. As teachers, we gamify our lessons, make learning hands-on, and experiment with cutting-edge tech, but it doesn't break through this apathy—not for the long term, anyway. That's because even the best strategies won't lead to transformative change if students are still tuned out.

To make history come alive in our classrooms, we must first make students come alive.

This book is about both of these goals. It offers a framework of active-learning strategies that you can use to help students build skills and master the content while firing you up to teach every day. The strategies—historical scavenger hunts, decision simulations, history labs, prediction bell work, Primary Source Sandwiches, and Socratic Smackdowns bridge the gap between fun and rigorous. It's about crafting learning experiences where students feel that the work they do matters, where they see the power and joy of learning history.

But this book is also about meeting students where they are and addressing the issues that hold them back from meaningful engagement. It's about getting reluctant learners to lean in and become curious. And it's about helping struggling learners develop confidence and resilience so they stop seeing failure or challenges as a dead end and start seeing them as part of the journey—a part that makes the learning worth it. It's about building a culture of curious learners who come into class wondering, *What do we get to explore today?*

This book is full of practical tools, activities, and strategies that have made a difference in my Title I public high school classroom. It's the framework I refined over sixteen years of teaching, experimenting, and failing forward lesson by lesson, unit by unit, until I had something that worked for me and my students. If you teach students who just don't seem to care no matter what you do, or if you're hungry to learn more ways to get students doing meaningful work that challenges them to think deeper about history and the world, then this book is for you.

Lectureless teaches how to move beyond the lecture as the default mode of instruction by laying out a framework that gets students *doing*, *experiencing*, and *learning from* history—not just learning *about* it. In science class, students conduct experiments in labs. In language arts, they write stories and poems. In art, they create, design, and make. In PE, students don't learn about dodgeball; they play dodgeball! So, in history class, why are students just learning *about* history instead of *doing* it? This book is about doing. It's about putting aside passive pedagogy for active learning—questioning, investigating, debating, and deciding.

The strategies in this book help students deepen their content knowledge, strengthen essential skills, and cultivate an appetite for civic engagement at a time when it's desperately needed.

And this book is not necessarily a call for all teachers to go 100 percent "lectureless." Lectures themselves aren't the enemy. Bad and lifeless lectures are. Lectures that leave students bored, uninspired, and waiting for the bell to save them from . . . one . . . more . . . slide.

A good lecture can be electric. It can pull students into the story, into the action, and it can hook them in a way few other strategies can. It can spark curiosity instead of smothering it. The same student who might tune out five minutes into a lecture might be glued to every twist and turn of an hour-long true crime podcast or a docuseries on Netflix. So, it's not the attention spans alone that's the problem—it's the execution. Some teachers are natural storytellers and keep students on the edge of their seats. Others are dynamic performers who bring history to life with passion and energy.

In chapter 3, I'll show you how to turn direct instruction into something more interactive and impactful—how to blend stories, performance, and active learning into lectures that help students learn *and* get them hungry to learn more. So while some teachers might use this book to go fully lectureless, others will simply learn how to lecture less but *better*.

Because even the best lecturers must still prioritize learning activities that let students wrestle with the past, struggle with ideas, and make meaning themselves. That's where the real learning happens—in the messy, frustrating, and exhilarating work of doing history. If we aim to develop our students into engaged and active citizens of the world, they first need to be engaged and active students in our classrooms.

Lastly, my hope is that this book ignites, or reignites, your passion for teaching and equips you with the tools and confidence to reach every student—even the most reluctant learners and the quiet, cautious ones, like Hope. It is my ultimate goal that this book helps you build a classroom where teaching and learning history feels like the great adventure it is.

Buckle up, teachers. Adventure awaits.

1

HISTORY'S NOT DEAD

Making the Past Relevant and Real

It's the first day of high school for my incoming freshman World History students. They shuffle into the room—some excited, some nervous, but most bracing for the usual monotony: syllabus review, class rules, maybe an awkward get-to-know-you icebreaker. Rinse and repeat for seven periods. But I have something else in mind.

At the door, I'm giving high fives and handshakes and pointing students to their seats. Bob Dylan's "Like a Rolling Stone" is blasting from my speakers. As they enter the room, students are confronted with our question of the day. It's written on the whiteboard in bold, sprawling letters: "Why should we care at all about learning history?"

I see their raised eyebrows, skeptical smirks, and curious glances. *Yeah, why should we?* It's a question every student has asked themselves but never seriously tried to answer. Before they even sit down, I've made it clear: We're not brushing this under the rug. In this class, we embrace those bold questions and dare to answer them.

What they don't know is that by the end of the period, it's going to be their job not just to answer the question but to convince me why history *does* matter.

The bell rings and I jet to the center of the room. "My name is Mr. Lewer. This is World History. And before we learn anything about the past, any dates or dead people, we are going to think about why the heck we are here and why we should care at all about history.

"Every civilization since the dawn of man has gone to incredible lengths to record and pass on their history. *Why?* For most of human history, only the privileged few had the sacred duty to learn and pass on the history of their people. *Why?* Today, every student in the United States is obligated by law to learn about the past. *But why?* Why waste our precious time studying and learning about the events and people who lived before us when we could be doing much cooler things, like playing video games or learning how to make a bunch of money?"

A few hands shoot up. "So history doesn't repeat itself?" Another student adds, "To learn from past mistakes?"

"Great responses! You're absolutely right, but we're going to dig a little deeper today."

This is the most important inquiry question we'll investigate all year. Why not lead off with it on day one?

"Today your work is to discover the most important reasons why studying history is not just worthwhile but potentially essential for our survival. You're going to start considering why history is perhaps the single most important thing we must learn if we hope to create a better, brighter future and live better, richer lives. Then we'll have a whole-class debate, and you're going to have to convince me of the most important reason why we must take the learning in this class seriously!"

And the crowd goes wild with excitement! I'm kidding. I wish that were the case, but what I get instead is wide-eyed, stunned silence.

This is not what students are expecting as they walk in on the first day of school, and that's partly the point. You cannot simply tell students, "*This* class is different, and we are going to do lots of fun, interesting activities here!" They've heard that too many times to believe it. You actually need to *show* them it will be different by making learning radical, dynamic, and unlike other classes they've had before. And yes, it starts on day one.

Trust me, the syllabus can wait. Going over how to submit late work or where to find the glue sticks can wait. Reviewing your rules, which are remarkably similar to the rules students have been asked to follow in every class for the past eight years, can wait.

Instead, start with a spark.

I have two goals for that first day of class. One is that students start to understand why history is awesome and that what we do in this class matters. And two is that all my students race to my class the next day asking themselves, *What are we going to get to do today?*

Do I achieve that second goal? Certainly not—but it's a worthy target to aim for.

The thing is, we have no choice but to give students the opportunity to explore why we study history. And that's because they're either already wondering why, or, worse, they're convinced it's a total waste of time. I'm a bit of a slow learner, so it took me about six years to realize that no matter how often I explained why history matters and passionately tried to convince students of how important it is, most just tuned it out.

Students are skeptical, and some are borderline cynical. Many are actually convinced that history is boring, useless, and (*gasp!*) totally irrelevant to their lives. Studying history is just something they *have* to do. Boxes to check off in order to graduate so they can leave history, well, in the past.

Then, I had a revelation. I was going to stop telling students why history matters.

I was going to have them tell me.

And it was going to start on day one.

Breakdown of My First-Day Activity

Across the classroom, I have six stations, each one with a different reason to study history. Here are the six reasons for my World History class:

1. History helps us better understand the world today.
2. Since history tends to repeat, learning history helps us solve future problems.
3. Learning about historical figures helps us become better people and live better lives.
4. Learning history can inspire us to make a difference in the world.
5. We are connected to people all over the world, so learning history helps us better understand one another.
6. Studying history helps us gain empathy and appreciation of our global diversity and its wondrous cultures.

For my US History course, I sub in these for numbers 5 and 6:

1. Knowing history helps us understand the roots of many of the conflicts our country faces today.
2. History helps us understand different parts of our country—our differences and what unites us as Americans.

In groups, students rotate through the stations, spending four minutes at each one discussing and recording their ideas on their answer sheets. The fast pace keeps the energy high and holds them accountable to make the most of their time. By the end of the activity, students have spent nearly thirty minutes grappling with meaningful ideas and engaging in rich conversations with their peers.

WHY STUDY HISTORY?		
PART I 1. As you go to each station around the room, copy the quote and then complete the questions with your partners.		
REASON TO STUDY TO HISTORY: Copy the quote.	**MEANING & REACTION:** What does this reason tell us is important about studying and learning history? How can it help YOU to learn history?	**RANKING:** Rank each one 1-6, which you think is the best reason to study history.
1.		
2.		
3.		
4.		
5.		
6.		

Next, they return to their desks for a mini debate with their groups, ranking the reasons to study history from most to least important. This primes them for the main event—the whole-class debate where students have to convince me and their peers that *their reason* is the single most important one. Students physically move to their station and then have to defend their arguments.

One year, I took it up a notch and got our vice principal into the mix. She told students that the school was considering cutting the history classes because they were a waste of time, unless she could be convinced otherwise. Students went to work trying to convince her why they needed to learn history and how it could help them in their lives. The VP was pleasantly won over and kept the courses. *Phew!*

By the end of that first lesson, students didn't just have an energizing and engaging first day; they thought deeply about the importance and relevance of history. Perhaps for the first time in their lives, they considered how past events and studying historical figures could help them in their lives. That beats the heck out of reviewing classroom procedures and covering the grading policy.

The Moral of the (Hi)Story

Even a home run on day one is not enough if you fall back into the routine of teaching history the same way it's always been taught. Students need regular opportunities to consider the importance of what they're learning and how it connects to their lives.

Without a direct connection to the past, history will always seem distant, abstract, and foreign. As it's said, the past is a foreign country. But when history is personal, it becomes meaningful and relatable.

SPARK CURIOSITY

Next time a student asks, "Why do we need to know this stuff?" applaud their skepticism. Show the class you invite bold, hard questions but challenge them to come up with the answers themselves!

At some point during each unit, you should challenge your students to find "the moral of the story." While history is no fairy tale with a clear moral for each topic, the point is to task students to consider what from the unit is most valuable, useful, or relevant to us today. What can we take away from this unit that actually matters to us living in the twenty-first century?

It might sound like this: "We've just explored the achievements of the Qin and Han dynasties—their contrasting approaches to power and their achievements in ancient China. But what's the point? What lessons can we take from their successes and failures that might matter in our lives or the world today?"

While we, as teachers, know there are a myriad of relevant lessons we can take from any unit or topic, our students don't, and they might not know it when they see it, if we never challenge them to look. If the point of history is to learn from our mistakes and make better decisions in the future, we must give students plenty of practice doing just that.

Four Prompts to Help Students See the Value of History

Looking for a no-prep activity to get students thinking deeply about the relevance of history? Try these simple but powerful prompts:

1. What is one thing from this unit that you learned that could help you become a better person?
2. "The most important lesson we must learn from [topic] to create a better world is ___________."
3. "If [topic] never happened, then ___________."
4. Imagine if [topic] was erased from history. What important lessons or ideas would the world miss out on?

If you teach reluctant and struggling learners, preparing for a discussion on the relevance of ancient Egypt or even the civil rights movement might be overwhelming. Some students will still give it their best shot, but others will tune out, believing the task is beyond their abilities.

A little scaffolding can go a long way in giving students the confidence and support they need to engage with big questions. That is what these prompts accomplish.

You can lower the stakes by having students answer the prompt with a "single original sentence." Even your most reluctant learners can manage that. It gives every student an entry ticket to the conversation, allowing ideas to start flowing and take shape, building momentum as it goes.

SPARK CONFIDENCE

The simplest questions sometimes spark the most profound discussions. Simple, open-ended questions lower the bar for entry but open the possibilities for exploration.

Time permitting, pause the discussion and have students turn their single sentences into a paragraph or two. The scaffold becomes a springboard, and round two of the discussion will get a lot juicier.

What We Can Learn from Mr. Miyagi and the Karate Kid

As a nineties child, I was raised on *The Karate Kid* movies. But when I rewatched the original recently, something in my teacher's brain clicked, and it changed how I thought about teaching history.

For the poor souls who don't already know, here's the basic plot: Daniel LaRusso is getting bullied and wants to learn self-defense. He asks the maintenance guy at his apartment complex, Mr. Miyagi, to teach him karate.

Except at first, Mr. Miyagi doesn't teach him karate at all. He has Daniel doing grunt work instead.

Daniel-san paints the fence. Daniel-san waxes the car. Daniel-san sands the floor. Daniel-san paints the house. After weeks of this, Daniel finally erupts on Mr. Miyagi, convinced he's not learning anything about karate.

He saw no value in these tasks, believing they were meaningless chores. This is the classroom equivalent of students believing their assignments are just busywork with no real value. Is it any surprise some of them just go through the motions or tune out altogether?

Then comes the big reveal.

Mr. Miyagi strikes at Daniel and tells him to "show me paint the fence" and the other movements he's practiced thousands of times. Daniel blocks every attack with the perfect defensive movement. At that moment, it clicks. He's been building muscle memory and learning the fundamentals of karate the entire time.

Without knowing it, Daniel *was* learning karate. And suddenly, all the tedious, seemingly meaningless work made sense. With that one lesson, he bought in. He saw the value and trusted the process.

That's when it hit me. We often tell students that history is important and that it will help them in the future. But we rarely give them opportunities to actually *use* it that way. Students need learning experiences that help them connect their lives to the distant worlds of our curriculum. They need chances to use history as a tool to address current events and conflicts.

Once they see the relevance, the engagement will follow. As Nietzsche stated, "He who has a why to live for can bear almost any how."

Let's take a page from Mr. Miyagi's pedagogy and give students the *why* they're desperate for.

Convince the Skeptic: A Gamified Debate on the Importance of History

I started this activity for my student Logan who just could never be convinced that history mattered at all. Everything I did to make learning relevant failed in his eyes (and he made sure to let the whole class know), so I leaned into his skepticism by creating an activity where he would be the star and the pest he was born to be.

Instead of a standard discussion on the lessons from the French Revolution, we had a gamified debate. The class broke into groups tasked with convincing Logan why it's essential to study the French Revolution. Groups had ten minutes to develop an argument for the most important lesson, *the moral of the story*, and then had to compete with one another to convince Logan why the French Revolution still mattered today.

The groups shared their opening statements before the debate began. Logan's job was to challenge their arguments and get them thinking deeper. Groups explored how good intentions can go awry, how allies can turn on each other when they don't have a common enemy, and how democracies and rights are fragile things. Things were getting heated as Logan found ways to shut down every argument until he finally quipped, "The only thing Napoleon teaches us is that we shouldn't trust guys with a Napoleon complex with that kind of power!" The class erupted in laughter until one student yelled emphatically, "*That's the point!*"

In the end, Logan had to choose the group that made the best argument and explain whether he was convinced. I feel pride made him say no, but he clearly loved the authority. It was such a hit that I started using it in my other classes as well.

SPARK ENGAGEMENT

Students love a challenge. By making a mundane task into a competition or game, you can make the learning more fun and exciting.

Bridges to the Present

It's not enough that our students learn *about* history; they need to learn *from* history. After all, that's what we tell our students, right? "We learn history so we don't make the same mistakes as in the past."

Worse than being a cliché, it's often not followed through with pedagogy. Because really, how often are we creating opportunities for students to apply the lessons from the past to pressing issues in the world today?

While we have an absurd amount of standards to get through in a year, it's important to carve out space for students to connect history to the present and their lives. Students might be generally skeptical about the value of history, but most teenagers are interested in understanding the world today.

Lean into that interest. That's where Bridges to the Present activities come in.

This simple, no-prep strategy gets students making connections between the past and the present. It helps them see history as a tool to understand issues we face today.

During my ancient India unit, students are always drawn to the Dalit, or untouchable, caste. Fascinated by their roles and the dehumanization these people faced, students really have their minds blown when we explore how Dalits live in India today.

NAME: ____________________

CASTE SYSTEM: THEN & NOW

Review & record what you have learned about the caste system in ancient India.	Record how the caste system impacts India today.
CASTE SYSTEM IN THE PAST	**CASTE SYSTEM TODAY**

IMPORTANT CHANGES	**IMPORTANT CONTINUITIES**

FINAL REFLECTION: IN A FEW SENTENCES, RECORD WHAT REALLY HIT YOU FROM THIS LESSON AND IF YOU ARE LEFT WITH ANY QUESTIONS.

With the Bridges to the Present sheet, we investigate this question: Is the caste system still shaping Indian society today?

Students read an article and watch a video about a Dalit man who became a millionaire yet still faces discrimination behind the wrought iron gates of his penthouse. This single lesson takes a system that's thousands of years old and makes it fresh, immediate, and relevant.

In our culminating discussion, some students share personal experiences with discrimination, others reflect on family pressure to carry on traditions, and some discuss how important religion is to them. By connecting their own lives to history and distant cultures, students begin to *see themselves* in the history and in the stories we are studying.

Suddenly, history is not some distant thing. It's not just something that happened but something that is still happening—that they are a part of and are participating in.

This is how we bridge history to the present.

This is how we get students to connect the dots from history to their lives.

This is how we get students learning *from* history and not just *about* history.

And that is empowering.

The Bridges to the Present template sets up an investigation lesson that can be used for almost any topic. The questions are open and inviting, allowing students more choice and voice in their investigations than they'd get with specific questions that lead to cookie-cutter responses.

SPARK ENGAGEMENT

The best discussions aren't about finding the "right" answer. They're about the clash of diverse ideas, perspectives, and questions that push everyone to think deeper.

Here are just a few of my favorite Bridges to Present investigations for my US History and World History classes. But you could pounce upon any major current event or pop culture trend. If it has students' attention and curiosity, bring it into class.

US History:

- Are President Washington's fears about political parties still relevant today?
- How is the AI revolution similar to the Industrial Revolution?
- Are we living in a second Gilded Age?
- Using lessons from the Cold War, what should the US policy toward the Russian invasion of Ukraine look like?

World History:

- How are medieval castles being used in Europe today?
- How would the totalitarian leaders of the 1930s have used social media to control their populations?
- Marvel vs. myth: How do Marvel superheroes compare to Greek gods?
- What has had a bigger impact on the world: the printing press or the internet?

Some of these are obviously more rigorous than others. Whether these are single lessons or a weeklong investigation, students will relish the opportunity to make historical connections to pop culture and the critical issues we face today. And gosh, isn't it a wonderful thing to be an educator helping students make sense of this complicated and crazy world?

Do activities like this somewhat regularly, and you will see students bring a different energy into class. When they walk into your room, they won't just expect to learn history. They'll expect to use it.

Historical Scavenger Hunts

If you want students to start seeing history as relevant, challenge them with seeing the history around them. Historical scavenger hunts challenge students to uncover connections and "living history" in the world today—on campus or out in their communities.

It's a surefire way to shake things up and energize students. Just say the words *cross-campus scavenger hunt* and watch them perk up, get curious, and begin itching for the challenge. You might even have students from your later classes running in to ask you, "Do we get to explore outside today?"

My first historical scavenger hunt wasn't planned—it was one of those magical, spontaneous teachable moments. While teaching the Industrial Revolution, I asked my students to look around the room and find things that were not made by machines—that were made entirely by hand and manpower.

They pointed to the murals that students painted on the walls, the handwritten essays that were hanging on the bulletin board, and a mug storing pens that a former student made in art class. But when I pressed them—"Where did the paint and brushes come from? What about the paper, the pens, or the clay?"—all those materials had been harvested and processed by machines.

That's when Leilani, a firecracker of a student, threw down a challenge. "I bet I can find ten things around campus that are *entirely* man-made," she said with a smirk.

That sounded like a teachable moment to me. "A homework assignment says you can't! But let's find out."

"Are you serious?" students asked.

"Heck yes!" I replied.

I called an audible on the lesson I had planned, and we took off on the adventure. As a class, we spent twenty minutes scouring the campus, looking for anything entirely man-made. Students pointed to some makeshift wooden benches, cement flowerpots, chicken wire recycle bins, and some jewelry the office ladies were wearing, but nothing *entirely* man-made. Students were dismayed.

But then . . . *treasure*!

In the Hawaiian studies classroom, we hit the jackpot: handwoven lauhala hats, gourd drums, dried flower leis, and even some taxidermy.

"All of this stuff is man-made, Mr. Lewer! Well, some of it was made by Auntie Holani, but still . . . That means we win the bet, Mr. Lewer. No homework, and I think you owe us some bonus points or something."

I applauded their discovery. While I thought the scavenger hunt was itself the prize, a few bonus points never hurt anyone.

Back in class, we pieced together the bigger picture. The only place we found entirely man-made items was in the Hawaiian studies room, a place dedicated to preserving culture and traditions that are . . . pre-industrial. The realization hit hard: Nearly every other part of our lives had been shaped by the Industrial Revolution.

Could I have found a better way to spend twenty minutes with my students to drive home the importance of our new unit? Not a chance. With our own little Corps of Discovery, looking for remnants of the past right on our campus, history came alive. And so did the students.

SPARK EXCITEMENT

There's no substitute for getting kids truly excited to learn. A few activities early in the year that shake things up and make learning fun will pay dividends all year long.

How to Do Historical Scavenger Hunts

1. Introduce the Activity

1. Explain to students that their goal is to find *living connections* to the historical topic being studied—evidence of how history has left its mark on their surroundings or how it connects to what you're learning in some way.

2. Provide some examples from other periods in history (so you're not giving away any gems that students can find on their own). Here are some examples from my Progressive Era scavenger hunt:
   - Fire alarms to reference the Triangle Shirtwaist Factory fire
   - The school garden for the conservation movement (this is a stretch but it works) Nutritional information on soda cans for the Pure Food and Drug Act

2. Set the Parameters

Assign students to small groups and give them fifteen to twenty minutes to hunt. Or go together as a class.

3. Snap a Picture

Instruct students to use their phones or Chromebooks to take photos of the connections they find.

4. Prepare a Presentation

Back in class, each group reviews their findings and selects the strongest or most unique example of a connection to the unit. They then prepare a one-minute presentation explaining how their item connects to the history being studied.

History Is All Around You

Historical scavenger hunts don't just get students thinking creatively and divergently about history. They don't just help learners have fun and build a positive connection to learning about history. They also start to build the habit of mind students need to see history as a living force in their daily lives.

And I know—there is not a standard for any of those things. But if it gets students looking forward to learning when they step into my classroom, I am going to make time for it. And how we get students hooked into the lesson in those first minutes of class is what we're diving into next.

We are teaching students, not standards. We are developing citizens, not subjects. And the exam that determines whether we were successful will not be multiple choice; it's who our students become after leaving our classrooms.

2

BELL WORK THAT WORKS

Hooking All Students in the First Three Minutes

It was 8:25 a.m. and the bell for first period had just rung. I headed to the door like normal, ready to greet students with my usual caffeine-fueled optimism. But something was off.

First, the moans from the hallway. Low, distant, guttural sounds. Growing louder.

Then, the smell. The teenage boys hadn't had PE yet, so it wasn't the normal BO masked by body spray. It was something worse. More foul and unsettling.

They came staggering past my door. Eyes glazed. Mouths slack. Bumping into lockers. Groaning. Heads glued to their phones or buried in Takis bags, dragging their limp bodies along.

Zach, my chipper VIP of period one, shuffled toward the door. I raised my hand for our usual high five. But he just bared his teeth and lunged at my arm. I stumbled back in shock and redirected him to his seat. Then I saw Kaysen, dragging himself across the floor, mumbling, "I forgot . . . my pencil . . ."

Within thirty seconds the room was overrun with adolescent undead. I panicked. We had drills for fires, active shooters, and in Hawai'i, even incoming missiles, but not . . . zombie attacks!

Grabbing the globe as a shield and the yardstick as a lance, I yelled, "Quick! Take out your notebooks. We're doing Cornell Notes on feudalism." Their groans were worse than normal.

Okay. I'm exaggerating. They weren't really undead.

But teenage-zombie mode is real. No craving for brains, just students running on little sleep, high anxiety, phone addictions, and a jaded outlook on the value of school and traditional education. These are students who are showing up physically for class, but mentally they're checked out. Slogging through the school day on autopilot. Going through the motions—and sometimes, just barely. Period after period. Lesson after lesson. Day after day.

That's why those first minutes of class are so important. It's your chance to shake them out of that zombie-like state and inject some energy and excitement into them. The moment students enter class provides this unique, wonderful opportunity to grab their attention, spark curiosity, and hook their interest. We only get one first impression for a lesson—let's make it count!

And it actually starts outside the class, before the bell rings. Be at the door giving high fives, cracking corny jokes, and most of all welcoming every student to class with a smile. Have music blasting. If the grumpy teacher next door is annoyed, you're doing it right. If you can, turn off those horrid overhead fluorescents and turn on the accent lights. And if you have windows, open them up and let the natural light pour in.

Projected at the front of the room, to grab students' attention, have a captivating image or powerful quote for their bell work. Get them raising an eyebrow or scratching their heads before they even take their seats.

This is my daily routine to shake students out of their zombie-like state. And it works. We may study the dead and gone, but my students sure as heck won't be half-alive while doing it. Because students feed off energy. If they see that you're excited to see them, that you're eager to teach, they'll be a heck of a lot more likely to be interested in learning. And their first task, the bell work, must be designed to build on this positive energy and hook them into the lesson.

Bell work is one of the smallest big things you can do to transform the learning community in your room. It's a routine that sets you and your students up for success each and every lesson. Done correctly, bell work is a daily opportunity to build students' confidence, curiosity, and critical thinking so "learning mode" is activated upon arrival. And because it's something you do every lesson, it has a compounding effect that you and the students will reap the benefits of throughout the year.

Those first three minutes are your chance to win the lesson. Make them count.

SPARK EXCITEMENT

There is no substitute for a teacher's passion. Students don't need a perfect teacher. They just need a teacher who is wildly enthusiastic and excited to teach and work with them each day.

Common Mistakes with Bell Work

For years I was doing bell work all wrong without even realizing it. And now that I get to work with and coach teachers, I see that it's one of the most common mistakes in classrooms that goes totally unnoticed.

Like many teachers, I used bell work primarily as a routine to settle students down and get them focused. The bell rings, students get to their seats, and they open their notebooks and complete a quick task. At first glance, it seems to work pretty well.

But here's what I was missing.

First, the bell work tasks were often review questions from the previous lesson. "What were three things you learned last class?" "Explain one effect of the Red Scare on American society." While recalling prior knowledge is absolutely essential, it is not the best way to get students fired up and jumping out of their seats to learn for the next forty-five or seventy minutes. It's unlikely to switch them off of autopilot and into high gear.

The bigger problem, though, was that my bell work left some students behind. First off, students absent from the last class couldn't engage. Worse, it was leaving behind struggling learners who might not recall much from the previous lesson—just as they were finding their seats.

Thus, frustration was meeting them at the door. Class had just started and they were reminded of how much they struggled in it. And to avoid struggling or "failing" with the warm-up, some would decide to act out to get positive attention from peers instead. And then I'd be redirecting students and putting out fires and the bell had only just rung.

This is no way to start class.

If struggling learners walk into class and can't even complete the bell work, the warm-up, the *give-me* question—they will start telling themselves stories you've heard before: "I'm stupid." "I don't get history." "This class is too hard." "I can't even do the warm-up!" And students tend to act out the stories they tell themselves.

That is why it's so important to help our struggling learners develop confidence in our classrooms. When students develop inner confidence and a sense of agency, they can begin to tell themselves a different story: "I *can* be successful when I try." "It might be hard, but I *can* do it." "History is actually kind of fun." These are the opening lines of a story that leads struggling learners to start meaningfully engaging in class. And the best part is they take that newfound confidence outside the four walls of our classrooms. It's a success they can build upon.

And last, the problem with most bell work tasks is that they're dreadfully boring. Sorry, but a quick recall task won't get kids fired up about the great lesson ahead. It's likely to be completed on autopilot with some students still asleep at the wheel.

SPARK CONFIDENCE

One of the greatest joys of teaching is helping students change how they see themselves. We have the power to take students who've never believed in themselves and get them to see their true potential.

Now let's imagine a bell work task that gets *all* students a win right off the bat, even those struggling learners and chronologically absent kids. And suppose that task gets them curious and interested in learning more about the lesson. Last, imagine that warm-up gets students to feel like they have skin in the game—a reason to pay attention and care about the lesson ahead.

Here's how you win those first three minutes.

Three-Part Framework for "All-In Bell Work"

I aim to accomplish three things with my bell work. But even if I hit two out of the three, I'm setting students and myself up for a great lesson. Here are the goals:

1. All students can successfully complete it to start with a win.
2. It sparks curiosity and interest in the topic.
3. It gets students to have skin in the game.

Let's unpack this a bit.

Start with a Win

If your bell work can be completed by all your students each day, it means they're starting with a win every time they come into your classroom. For struggling learners, this is no small thing. It can help to build their confidence and their willingness to engage in the rest of the lesson.

And if the whole class starts off moving in the right direction together, day after day, it does wonders to improve the learning culture in the room. Compare this with starting with 15 percent of your students struggling, getting off task, and needing to be redirected.

The choice is clear.

Spark Curiosity

Meeting students at the door with high fives, blasting music related to the topic (whenever possible), and projecting a captivating historical image on the screen with a simple but stimulating challenge—with these strategies, I'm pulling students into a unique learning space right as they step into my room. The quick task is designed to pique their interest and get the wheels turning. The goal isn't to blow their minds; it's just to get them scratching their heads or raising an eyebrow.

> SPARK CURIOSITY
>
> **Curiosity is the lifeblood of engagement. It's the wind in the sails of any lesson. Without curiosity, it's just compliance.**

Get Skin in the Game

Sometimes students don't pay much attention to the lessons (even when they're doing the work—have you noticed that?) because they feel there's really nothing in it for them. They are checking off boxes. Doing chores.

That's why I want students to get some skin in the game with bell work. With the tasks I share below, I get students to make a small investment in the lesson by having them guess what they're about to learn. It gives them something to win or lose, which creates an incentive to focus and pay attention during the lesson. It gets them to give a damn.

So how do we do this within the first three minutes of class? Here are some of my favorite bell work tasks.

Prediction Bell Work

One of the best ways to start class is with a prediction bell work. To do this, turn the learning goal for the lesson into a question, set the scene with a bit of context, include a juicy image, and let students guess what happens next or what led up to this moment.

If the learning goal is "I can explain the effects of Columbus's landing in the Americas," a prediction bell work prompt might look something like this:

"It is 1492. Christopher Columbus and nearly a hundred Spanish explorers just arrived on a small island in the Americas. They are about to encounter a Native American tribe and neither group—the Spanish nor the Americans—have any knowledge of the other. What do you predict happens next when they start interacting?"

Notice how the scenario thrusts them into the past: "It *is* 1492 . . ." The setup builds tension, the image adds depth, and right away, history feels more immediate—something unfolding in front of them. It pulls them into the story.

SPARK EXCITEMENT

The simplest way to immerse students in history is by changing the frame of how you teach a topic. Instead of looking back at an event, challenge students to consider experiencing it firsthand as a historical figure. We all want to be the main character—with our lessons, we can at least let them pretend.

Even if a student has been absent or knows exactly zilch about the Age of Exploration, they can still take a logical guess at what could happen next. Thus, all students can start with a win. *Check.*

After they jot down predictions, call on some students to share aloud with the class. Record their predictions on the board so students have visual reminders during the lesson.

Here are the predictions that generally come up for this lesson:

- They start trading.
- A war breaks out.
- The Spanish will spread Christianity (this student remembered the three Gs (God, gold, and glory as a main motivator for European exploration) from the last lesson).
- They form an alliance.
- The Spanish start building homes and villages.
- The Native American tribes try to drive the Spanish away.

And here's an example of what I'll say after we've finished our predictions: "Great predictions, class! I bet some of these are right, but let's find out! We're going to read a textbook excerpt and an entry from Christopher Columbus's journal to discover what happened in the days and weeks that followed. As you read, if you discover your prediction was correct, go up and put a checkmark next to your guess on the board."

Do you think students are going to be a little more interested in the reading? Do you think they're going to be able to make better sense of what might otherwise be a challenging primary source? *Of course!* Because they're going into the reading with a purpose and with gears already turning in their brains. They are now more curious and have skin in the game. *Check* and *check*.

And you know the bell work hits when you hear students exclaiming, "I knew it!" or "Wow! Keanu called it!"

There's one more thing that this bell work does to improve learning outcomes. While simply writing a learning target on the board to appease administrators accomplishes nothing, students do benefit from knowing what they're trying to learn and accomplish in the lesson. They're much more likely to hit a target if they know where to aim. It gives them direction and focus to help them navigate and make sense of what they're learning.

And if there's a better way to do that then with a prediction bell work, I haven't seen it.

Exit Pass

Want some closure for the lesson so it comes full circle? A great exit pass for this lesson is to have students revisit their predictions and improve upon them. Were they correct? If so, they can add examples or specific terms to demonstrate what more they learned. If they were off, they can explain what actually happened using a vocab term or two.

For more examples of prediction bell work, scan this QR code.

Notice, Wonder, Think

Sometimes simplicity is the best pedagogy. And Notice, Wonder, Think is a simple strategy that packs a serious punch. While it is not exclusively a bell-work strategy, because it is designed to spark curiosity in a topic, it works wonderfully as that opening hook.

This routine was first developed by Ron Ritchart and the researchers at Harvard Graduate School of Education's Project Zero. They use *See, Think, Wonder*, and, though I made slight modifications, the goal is to encourage close observation, analysis, and to spark curiosity.

A great Notice, Wonder, Think starts with a captivating image. Photographs, advertisements, political cartoons, propaganda posters, works of art, and photos of historical artifacts all work wonderfully. Project the image as large as you can to grab students' attention and get them scratching their heads right as they walk through the door.

When introducing Buddhism to my World History & Cultures students, I use this image.

Do you think this gets students curious about just what the heck is happening in this photograph? *Uh, yeah!*

Alongside whatever image you use, include these three prompts:

- Notice: What do you notice that seems interesting or important?
- Wonder: What is a question you have about the image?
- Think: What do you think is going on here?

Notice how low-risk and inviting these questions are. This is a great confidence builder for your struggling learners, but the prompts are open enough for your more advanced learners to take their thinking deeper. They might notice symbolism in the image, their questions might connect to other topics you've studied, and they might be able to more accurately predict the story the image is telling.

As with all bell work in my classes, after students answer the prompts, they discuss their responses with their elbow partners and then as a whole class. The image sparks a conversation about meditation, nonviolence, colonialism, and reincarnation. But most importantly, it gets them curious to learn more.

Spending five minutes analyzing one image serves to crystallize it into what I call an anchor image. As you go through the lesson, you can remind students of different parts of the image to make abstract ideas and concepts more concrete. Chances are they'll remember this image weeks or even months later, helping to make the lesson and the concepts stick.

And if a bell work task not only hooks students into the lesson but also helps them make sense of what they learn, it's a heck of a way to spend the first few minutes of class.

Exit Pass

A great exit pass for a lesson that starts with a Notice, Wonder, Think is to challenge students to "tell the story" of that anchor image using evidence from what they learned during the lesson. Rather than just writing a summary of a few facts, this brings the lesson full circle to help students make meaning of what they learned.

Novel, Silly, and Fun Ways to Start Class

If laughter is the best medicine, it's also damn good pedagogy. While our goal is serious academic rigor and character development, humor is a means to those ends. Even high school students need space to be a little silly, and if you can get them laughing with their warm-up task, they're likely to lean into the lesson.

And let's face it. History can be downright depressing, dark, and horrifying—so lightening things up on occasion is a must. Just use your own professional discretion to not trivialize or make light of sensitive topics.

Image Alive

Here's a challenge for you. Complete this bell work task and fill in the thought bubbles for our coal miner friends.

"Breaker boys, Woodward coal mines." Detroit Publishing Company. 1900.

Were your answers silly or serious? The photograph lends itself to both, right?

Now imagine students walked into your class and this was the task awaiting them. Do you think they'd get interested in child labor and working conditions in the industrial age? Do you think they might be curious about what these kids' lives were *actually* like?

That's the point! Remember, one of the primary goals of bell work is to get students just curious enough that they have an interest in the topic they previously never thought about. An ounce of curiosity, a pound of engagement.

I call this activity Image Alive, and it's as simple as adding thought bubbles or dialogue boxes to get students interacting with still images. With PowerPoint, Google Slides, or Canvas, this can be done in seconds with a click of a button.

To complete this task, students need to carefully study the picture. They need to look for clues and break down different parts of the image to piece together a story of their lives. Students need to put themselves in the shoes of those child laborers and practice historical empathy in the process. So while their answers might be silly, this activity still requires serious analysis.

Laughter does wonders to build community and connection in the classroom. If your learners are suffering from learning fatigue or historical onset depression, apply humor liberally to your lessons.

SPARK EXCITEMENT

Host a "dad joke competition" to close out class one day. Put students in groups and challenge each to develop one corny, silly, or ridiculous joke related to the topic of the lesson. Most will be absolutely terrible, but if one great joke is shared, the whole class will erupt in laughter and the joke writer will be a hero for days.

What Do You Meme?

Tap into student interests by embracing a little meme culture in your classroom. With this bell work strategy, challenge students to create either a hashtag or a meme for a historical image. By offering a choice, you ensure that all students can participate successfully—whether they enjoy crafting witty meme captions or prefer summarizing the image with catchy hashtags.

For example, you might project an image of exhausted factory workers from the Industrial Revolution or soldiers in a muddy trench during World War I. Some students might caption the factory photo with "When you asked for a raise and got 16-hour shifts instead," while others could opt for hashtags like #NoDaysOff or, for the trench warfare photograph, #MudLife.

Afterward, share responses as a class. This builds community and interest in the topic. Why were factory conditions so terrible? What made trench warfare so grueling? With their interest piqued, students are primed to dive into the lesson eager to discover more.

The moment students enter our classrooms, we have this wonderful opportunity to grab them by their brains, awaken them, and get the whole class on board moving forward together.

If history is a story, those first three minutes should get students asking one question: "What happens next?"

3

LECTURE LESS BUT BETTER

"I only lecture on the days I'm not prepared to teach."

That line hit like a slap across the face during one of my first PDs as a new history teacher. It stuck with me for years, echoing in the back of my mind when planning out lessons. I knew the lecture was not the only way we instruct, but wasn't it a core component of teaching history? That quote and training made me think otherwise, and I worked to lecture as little as possible in my classes during my first few years. I would rush through direct instruction with guilt so we could get to the *real* learning. But that guilt eventually gave way to something more useful: clarity. It's not that lectures are inherently bad—it's that some lectures are bad. And some of mine definitely were.

I'm not alone in seeing the lecture as an outdated practice. It's been on the chopping block for decades. It's often vilified for being the epitome of teacher-centered, passive learning. You know the cliché. The teacher stands in the front of the room clicking through slides while students sit quietly, scribbling notes, droning in and out of consciousness. Cue the Ferris Bueller reference.

But just because *some* lectures, and lecturers, are boring and ineffective, it doesn't mean they all are. Like all strategies, it depends on the execution. Cue the King Henry VIII joke.

Done correctly, a lecture can be dynamic, impactful, and even interactive. And lectures can lead to what matters more than anything: lasting learning and understanding.

So this chapter (and book) isn't a call to eliminate lectures entirely. It's a call to lecture with intention, purpose, and passion. It's a call to lecture *less* but *better*. The lecture is one tool in our history teacher's toolbox, and it still has a place in our pedagogy if used effectively. And for those looking to go completely lectureless, this chapter breaks down ways to weave short and focused direct instruction into active-learning strategies that will elevate engagement and improve learning outcomes.

The Lecture as an Enticement

When I step in front of the class to lecture, the goal isn't to dump content into my students' brains. It's not to make up ground or keep up with the pacing guide. If that's the goal, you're setting up a lecture that students will endure rather than remember.

The lecture can be an effective tool of instruction, but maybe more important than covering content is the capacity for direct instruction to get students excited about the material. While a lecture can help introduce and make sense of new terms, ideas, and concepts, their power lies in their ability to pique students' curiosity.

The best lectures don't try to do it all or cover every standard. They teach the essentials while sparking a sense of wonder and highlighting the big picture—the stakes, the drama, or why it matters. When a lecture ends, the goal isn't for students to know everything about the topic but for them to want to know more.

SPARK EXCITEMENT

Too much of a good thing gets boring quick. You want students begging for more—another round of Blooket, another few minutes to work on a project, another one of your stories before the bell.

When lecturing, I'm trying to open a story, not close it. I want students leaning in, wondering what happens next—not zoning out while I march them through a parade of bullet points. By setting the stage and the stakes, students can move forward into the learning activity with eagerness.

It's my belief that direct instruction is absolutely necessary to clarify concepts and help students make meaning of what they've learned throughout a lesson or activity. In a student-centered classroom, where students take the driver's seat for much of the lesson, brief lectures after learning activities can be essential to help students stitch together details and bring the big picture into focus. As the expert in the room, you can use direct instruction to bring appropriate closure and understanding.

And one of the best ways to improve a lecture is to stop thinking like a lecturer and start thinking like a storyteller.

The Need for Narrative Maps

A narrative is not just helpful—it's essential for students trying to make sense of the past. But it has limits. A standard lecture, much like a textbook, often offers a single narrative, and no single narrative can capture the full complexity of history. Thus, it flattens the past.

At the same time, without any narrative at all, students are left trying to make sense of disconnected events with no structure to guide them.

In that way, narratives are like maps.

Every map distorts reality. A three-dimensional world flattened onto a page always loses something. Just ask a geographer about the Mercator projection and you'll see how spicy this issue is. Still, without maps, we'd be lost. So we use them but take into account their biases and distortions.

We should use narratives and stories the same way.

In student-centered history classrooms, where the burden of meaning-making is placed on the student, providing a clear narrative (even if it's at the end of the lesson, after students have worked through the material themselves), might be one of the most important roles of direct instruction. It provides students with a point of reference—a frame to organize and clarify their own ideas and something to compare their own interpretations against.

With that foundation, students can deepen their understanding, add greater nuance, and even challenge the narrative itself.

Just as maps help us navigate the world, narratives help students navigate the past.

Story Lectures

If you want to cover content quickly, use drill-and-kill lectures. If you want the content to stick, tell a story.

There's a reason why every culture since the dawn of man has passed down creation stories. If they'd passed down creation lectures instead, nobody would have stayed awake long enough to remember them.

But seriously—creation stories, like all stories, convey important lessons in a way that even children can process, remember, and make use of. We are hardwired for stories. As author Salman Rushdie said, "When a child is born, the first thing the child requires is safety and love. The next thing the child asks for is 'Tell me a story.'"

Stories *are* how we make sense of the world, and they're one of the most effective ways to teach and move an audience. Civilizations pass down their histories with stories. Marketers in commercials don't present facts and details; they craft stories about their products. Lawyers don't simply present evidence at trials; they use the evidence to construct a narrative to sway the jury. In his captivating TED Talks, Hans Rosling brings population data to life by using stories to make sense of graphs and charts. And if Rosling can make demographic data high drama through storytelling, you can surely do the same for Genghis Khan, the ancient Greeks, or World War II.

And here's the best news: We have the greatest stories in human history at our fingertips. No matter how dull or complicated you find a topic, it's full of conflict, ambition, betrayal, triumph, and failure. It's all right there waiting to bring your content to life. Stories humanize content. They give meaning to facts, relevance to dates, and emotion to events. They help students connect the dots and remember what matters. And that's why we should ground lectures in stories: because it pulls students into the history and the lessons it offers. After all, it's not called his*facts* or his*lectures*—its hi*story*. It's in the name of our discipline, for goodness' sake!

Three Ways to Teach with Stories

TELL PERSONAL STORIES THAT RELATE THE TOPIC OR THEME OR THAT CONNECT TO THE LESSON. Ever notice how students sometimes try to waste class time by getting you to tell them stories from your life? Why not lean into that and make your stories part of the lesson?

When I introduce the Cuban Missile Crisis, I don't start with Kennedy, Castro, or Khrushchev. I start with hide-and-seek. That was my favorite game when I was a kid. And at seven years old, I found my all-time best hiding spot at my grandparents' house.

Their basement had a creepy lower cellar. Tribal masks and abstract art hung on the walls. It was dark and damp, with thick cement walls and floors that were as cold as ice. And in the back of the cellar, where I was too afraid to venture alone, were wooden shelves stacked with canned foods—tomatoes, peaches, beans, and who knows what else.

One day, though, when playing hide-and-seek with my grandpa, I faced my fears in search of the perfect hiding spot. I walked down into the lower cellar, headed to the back, and climbed to the third and top shelf. I rearranged a dozen or so cans of green beans and took refuge behind them. I heard the call from upstairs: "Ready or not, here I come!"

From the safety of my tin fortress, I waited. And waited.

For nearly ten minutes, but what felt like forever, my grandpa searched every inch of the basement and cellar. When he finally surrendered, I climbed down—giddy with excitement, grinning ear to ear. "Nice one, Danny-boy! Knowing how you feel about green beans, I never would have looked there," he said laughingly.

"Grandpa, why do you have so many cans of beans, cranberries, and all this food down here?"

He paused, and his demeanor grew more serious. He was a World War II veteran and loved telling war stories. "Well, back when your mom was about your age, we were really scared of a war with Russia. If there was a war, it was going to be a frightful one due to the new weapons being developed. Families built cellars like this one. Thick concrete walls"—he knocked on a wall, producing a hollow thud—"to keep us safe in case the bombs ever dropped. We had enough food to last us a full year down here."

A pretty heavy thing to lay on a seven-year-old, but all I thought at the time was *Holy moly! That's so cool!*

This story brings abstract concepts from the Cuban Missile Crisis to life for my students. Suddenly the Cold War is not just about political posturing and military strategy but about fear, survival, and personal choices that real families made.

One year, after telling this story, my student Jada said, "I sometimes forget that history happened to real people." We had done simulations, watched videos, read primary sources, but this is what made history real for Jada. That's the power of a story.

You have a whole archive of stories from your personal life that you can draw from to make abstract concepts tangible for your students. Even little anecdotes can work wonders.

I tell the story of eating Indian food at my friend Ankur's house to connect to my spice trade lesson. I share the story of going to a WWE wrestling event in Madison Square Garden to make connections to the Roman Colosseum. And I tell students about cutting my hand on a meat slicer while working at my dad's pizzeria to connect to the dangers of factory work in the industrial age.

Let your stories be a gateway for students to access the past.

TELL HISTORICAL STORIES AND BRING LIFE TO THE DUSTY, DRY FACTS OF A STANDARD LECTURE. Kids don't connect with history until they connect with the people who lived it. Great stories are built on great characters. So, to get students more interested in history, zoom in. Bring the characters' personas, quirks, ambitions, love interests, and dramas to life with your lectures. In short, spill the tea.

Love him or hate him, one cannot help being fascinated by Andrew Jackson. Stories of Jackson color my entire antebellum unit.

To illustrate the Age of the Common Man, I share the story of the "inaugural brawl," where tides of ruffian Jackson supporters descended on the Capitol to celebrate his presidency, culminating in a full-on White House rager. Drunken supporters filled the rooms, broke furniture, and spat tobacco juice on the carpet, and it only ended when someone lured them outside with spiked punch.

I tell students about Jackson's dueling escapades, his interest in hanging his own vice president, and how a failed assassination attempt on the aging president ended with Jackson beating the would-be assassin senseless with his cane. When parents retell these stories to me at back-to-school nights, I get the feeling the lessons are resonating with the kids.

You don't need a PhD to tell great historical stories. Documentaries, history podcasts, and even your textbook are goldmines for juicy anecdotes you can share in class. And you can check out my YouTube channel, History for Humans, which uses the story-lecture model in each episode. Build your bank of stories and draw on them to make units more colorful and dramatic.

READ CHILDREN'S BOOKS TO YOUR CLASS TO MAKE ABSTRACT CONCEPTS RESONATE. Even if your secondary students pretend to be too cool for school, they'll still appreciate a classic story-time reading. Lean into the nostalgia by pushing away the desks and having students sit on their notebooks as you read a children's story to them.

"Criss-cross, applesauce! Hands in your lap. It's story time, class!"

Sure, some students will roll their eyes, but they'll be hooked before the story is through. And they'll remember it too.

Dr. Seuss has great ones for history classes:

- *The Butter Battle Book* can help you teach about the arms race.
- *The Lorax* is great for the environmental movement.
- *Yertle the Turtle* is a good pick for fascism.

Here are some other classics:

- *If You Give a Mouse a Cookie* by Laura Joffe Numeroff is great for prewar appeasement.
- *The True Story of the 3 Little Pigs!* by Jon Scieszka can really drive home how bias and point of view influence sources.

And trust me, students will be laughing their butts off at *President Taft Is Stuck in the Bath* by Mac Barnett.

And if you want to switch things up, have students *write* their own children's books about a historical event or figure. Instead of another essay, this pushes them to break down complex ideas and look for the silver lining of historical topics in a way that's clear, engaging, and fun. If they can explain the Gilded Age or the Cold War in a way a six-year-old would understand, they actually *get it.*

SPARK CURIOSITY

Classrooms should be ecosystems of wonder where students are free to dream, imagine, and create. Serious academic rigor should be balanced with playful curiosity, delight, and a touch of whimsy.

Question-Driven Lectures

The problem with the traditional lecture, fundamentally, is it's telling students the answers to questions they never cared to ask. The teacher steers. The students follow. But with a simple tweak, students can shift from passive passengers to active participants.

The key is to get them asking questions first. Spark curiosity before you start shuffling through slides. When students generate the questions, they're far more likely to be invested in the answers.

It might sound like this.

"Class, I'm going to get things started today with a brief lecture on the causes of the French Revolution. In the next twenty minutes, you're going to learn why the French people made the radical decision of overthrowing their king, whose family ruled over France for over *two hundred years*, to create a whole new government. But first, I want you to come up with a question or two about our topic: the causes of the French Revolution." (There'll be much more on *how* to get students asking quality questions in chapter 7.)

Give students a couple of minutes to brainstorm with elbow partners or table groups. Then, call on volunteers to share. In just a few minutes, you've transformed the lecture from a passive monologue into inquiry-driven instruction.

During the lecture, you can highlight and celebrate students' questions as they're answered. But what about the unanswered questions? Well, you could go off-road a bit to answer these questions, or you could build suspense by holding off if they'll be answered later in the lesson. Or, if students are really determined, have them research the question on their own time and report back to class what they discovered.

But I plead with you: Don't let the fear of not answering all student questions hold you back from using this strategy. Too many unanswered questions is a wonderful problem to have! We should be so lucky to have students asking more questions than we can answer. For myself, I'm much more worried about getting to the end of the lecture or lesson and finding students have no questions at all. That's a sign of compliance. And that is the death knell of curiosity and active learning.

SPARK CURIOSITY

When the classroom is filled with more questions than answers, we're creating a culture of curiosity and the conditions for true learning.

By bringing student questions into the lecture, direct instruction becomes more than just a one-way conversation. And with more students actively participating, the lecture becomes more impactful.

Interactive Lectures

A great lecture weaves in opportunities for students to talk, doodle, and, occasionally, even move. For most secondary students, every five to seven minutes of content delivery should be followed by an opportunity to process. If we expect students' undivided attention during lectures, they'll need opportunities for engagement beyond note-taking and head nodding.

Wiki-Chats: Fast-Paced Processing Activities

My go-to processing activity during a lecture is wiki-chats. Not to be confused with the chatbot, these are essentially think-pair-shares except my students think *wiki-chats* sounds cooler, so for marketing purposes, wiki-chats it is.

A great wiki-chat should help students review the material while energizing them. Here are some examples:

- Simple review—"With your table partners, list three achievements of the Qin dynasty."
- Hypothesis—"Why do you think Shihuangdi sought to expand the Great Wall of China?"
- Debate—"Have a quick debate on which dynasty was more important for Chinese history—the Qin or Han? The student closest to the bookcase will argue for the Han, and the student closer to the board will argue for the Qin. You have ninety seconds. Go!"
- Image analysis—"Carefully study the projected image. With your partner, discuss the questions below and be ready to

share with the class in one minute." (Quieter classes benefit from an image to guide their discussions.)

- Sketch and guess—"On your whiteboards, create a sixty-second sketch of one concept or term from your notes. See if your neighbor can guess what it is."
- Movement break—"Stand up and push in your chairs. Go find a 'solemate' (a peer with similar footwear) and answer the projected question in thirty seconds." And after: "Now, go find your 'shirtmate' and answer the new question."
- Snowball quiz—"On your Post-it, create one quiz question about something from the lecture notes. Now, crumple it into a 'snowball' and toss it across the room. Grab one, find a partner, and answer the questions together." (This is a great one when the lesson needs an injection of laughter.)
- Movie title—"If this topic were a Hollywood movie, what would you title it? With your partner, come up with a catchy, bold title that would make people want to buy tickets to see it!" (This one is done at the end of the lecture.)

These brain breaks can be one to four minutes long. Even the quicker, simpler ones will help students stay engaged and better understand the material. Careful with the more dynamic ones, though—students might start requesting more lectures.

Nearpod and Pear Deck

Embedding review or critical thinking tasks into a lecture has never been easier thanks to these two interactive tools for slide presentations. Nearpod and Pear Deck are extensions to Google Slides and PowerPoint, and they have a plethora of premade processing tasks and assessment tools that integrate right into a slide deck, including mapping practice, timelines, matching, vocab reviews, quiz questions, polls, doodling, and much more. Every slide can become interactive to keep students actively engaged as you lecture.

Best of all, these give you instant feedback on what students are learning (or not learning) in real time, so you can adjust as needed.

Lecture Like You Love It

Since the majority of time in my classroom is spent on student-centered activities and investigations, when I do lecture, I go all out. By channeling every ounce of energy, passion, and theatrical flair into the instruction, I hope that even the most apathetic students grow interested—if not in the topic, at least in the performance.

Because if you're not loving the lecture that you're delivering, your students certainly won't be. If you're just rushing to get through it, students will know it. Shakespeare said the whole world is a stage, and for us teachers, the whole classroom is our stage. So ditch the podium and command the room.

And get students moving, too, when you can. This can help you emphasize key points. Gather them in the front of the room to show them the fine details of an image or huddle them up, *Dead Poets Society* style, to share the climax of a story. Call on volunteers to re-create an image in the slideshow so you can point out the details on your live subjects, making history three-dimensional.

Most importantly, to really command the room, you have to always be reading the room. You need your finger on the pulse of student attention. Students' body language, facial expressions, and energy levels tell you everything—if they're following along, if they're lost or confused, if they're locked in or about to crash out. This helps you gauge when to push forward, pivot to a brain break, or call an audible. Remember, you're not teaching standards; you're teaching students. The goal of the lecture is not to get through the content. It's to get the lesson through to your students.

Lectures still have a place in the history classroom when they're done with purpose and passion. When they spark curiosity instead of smothering it. When they pull students into the story, make the characters and the drama come to life, and get students not just understanding the material but hungry to get their hands on it.

SPARK EXCITEMENT

You can't teach passion, but you can inspire it. If we want eager and excited students, we need to bring positive energy to our teaching and radiate a love of learning.

4

PRIMARY SOURCES

Bring Historical Texts to Life

We were an hour into our analysis of the most challenging primary source of the year, Maximilien Robespierre's "On Political Morality" speech. Students were trying to figure out why Robespierre believed the use of terror was necessary to protect the revolutionary government in France. For my ninth graders, many of whom were struggling readers, this took serious close reading, and rereading. And re-rereading.

I was not their favorite person that day.

Back in August, many of these students thought reading more than a single paragraph beyond their grade level was a violation of the Geneva Conventions. By the third quarter, I had built up their tolerance for academic reading, but this was still a big ask.

To combat decoding fatigue that I knew would set in at some point, I had done all I could to hook them into the lesson—a massive guillotine was drawn on the whiteboard, two bloody prop crowns were laying in a little basket of white linen just below the drawing, a banner reading "Liberté, Egalité, Fraternité" waved from my podium, and a French café station was playing on Spotify as students entered class.

It was working—at first. Students were busy in their reading groups highlighting, annotating, and trying to break down the speech, piece by piece. However, they just couldn't fully grasp Robespierre's main argument: how terror and virtue were symbiotic forces during the revolution.

After nearly an hour of this, some students were giving up. Discussions quieted, and groups were shaking their heads at the reading like it had personally wronged them. But I felt they were so close to getting it, so I pushed them to keep going.

"Class, you're almost there, let's reread this paragraph one more time and try to make sense of it with your groups." With a terrible French accent that almost sounded Italian, I read, "If the mainspring of popular government in peacetime is virtue, amid revolution it is at the same time [both] virtue and terror: virtue, without which terror is fatal; terror, without which virtue is impotent. Terror is nothing but prompt, severe, inflexible justice; it is therefore an emanation of virtue. It is less a special principle than a consequence of the general principle of democracy applied to our country's most pressing needs."

Though not in its original French, this was still a foreign language for most of my freshmen. Exasperated, Sean said, "Mr. Lewer, help a brother out, and just tell us what he means."

SPARK CONFIDENCE

Great teachers set a high bar for students and balance it with support, patience, and flexibility to get them to meet it. It's not enough to believe in our students. We must get them to believe in themselves.

Feeling defeated, I was about to give them the answer when Kiara raised a shaky hand. "Is he saying that they need, like, a Batman to protect the revolution?"

Confused, I asked her to say more. She continued, "We were talking about how Gotham has their normal police and politicians and stuff—that's kind of like the virtue he's talking about, but they aren't able to stop the Joker by following the rules, so they have to call on Batman. He doesn't follow those rules—he does what needs to be done even if it's not 'virtuous.' That is like how Robespierre thinks France needs to use terror to rid the country of the enemies of the revolution. Is that what he's saying, the guillotine was, like, the French Batman?"

The whole class was stone silent. Then—*boom*! They lit up. "Yeah!" Sean yelled. "The *Dark* Knight! Terror is going to protect the revolution like Batman protects Gotham! Sometimes blood needs to be spilled, right?"

I don't know if I had ever experienced a full-class, collective aha moment until then. As teachers, we live for those—but for that one, I could have died. Kiara's Batman connection helped the whole class understand the Reign of Terror and Robespierre's speech better than any lecture, any textbook, any worksheet ever could. Her metaphor was the key that unlocked the whole text for the class.

And what really made that aha moment so powerful was the nearly sixty minutes students had spent struggling to analyze and make sense of the text. But even for classes that don't have that crystallizing moment of understanding, analyzing challenging historical documents provides educational rewards that other learning activities simply cannot. Primary sources can be frustrating and intimidating, but that's exactly why they belong in our classrooms. They pull students into the past, challenging them to wrestle with history on its own terms. More than textbook overviews, students need opportunities to engage directly with the speeches that changed the world, analyze art that pushed the boundaries of human expression, and step inside the minds of history's great leaders, thinkers, and dreamers.

When they do, they are not just learning history—they are entering and uncovering it. And that ownership makes all the difference.

Primary Sources and Time Machines

As opposed to secondary sources like textbooks, documentary films, and lectures, primary sources are the raw, unfiltered accounts of the past. Letters, speeches, political cartoons, laws, propaganda posters, protest songs, diary entries, campaign buttons, and bullet shells. Instead of reading *about* history, students get to read *into* it when they use primary sources.

In my romantic teacher's brain, studying primary sources transforms my classroom into a time machine, transporting my class into the age and place we are studying. "That is not the door to room E10 you walked through; you just entered a portal to Paris, France, in 1793, citizen!" As Carl Sagan, the great astrophysicist and educator, said, "One glance at a book and you hear the voice of another person, perhaps someone dead for a thousand years." And when you dive deep into a primary source, you don't just hear their voice—you step into their world and become witness to their times.

You enter the action.

A decade ago, at a training led by Bruce Lesh, author of *"Why Won't You Just Tell Us the Answer?": Teaching Historical Thinking in Grades 7–12*, he described analyzing primary sources as "dancing with the dead." And if there's a better way to sell reading primary sources to students, I haven't heard of it.

As I like to announce, "Take out your highlighters, pens, and dust off your dancing shoes because we're dancing with the dead today! Let's see how well you and General Washington can shake a leg!"

SPARK ENGAGEMENT

Changing the language of how you present a lesson can make a huge difference in how students perceive, and thus engage, with the task. We don't "*have* to read today," we "*get* to read today." Learning is a privilege, not a chore, and our language must communicate that.

The Ken Burns Classroom Effect

One way I try to create a more immersive learning experience when using primary sources is with what I call the Ken Burns classroom effect. If you're reading this, I am assuming two things—you are a history teacher and you adore the documentary film director and national treasure Ken Burns. If either of those is untrue, we can no longer be friends. Please return this book and unfollow me on Instagram.

But since that's not the case, you probably know Burns's pioneering method of bringing historical images to life with what has been dubbed the Ken Burns effect. By zooming or panning across an image, Burns makes still images appear to be moving pictures. He also layers music into the background—either from the era or to fit the mood, occasionally while someone reads a primary source to "shake the image to life," in Burns's words.

I try, however poorly (and on a teacher's budget), to replicate that magic in my classroom. When reading a primary source, I like to project an anchor image on the screen and whenever possible, play light background music that matches the mood or the time period. The image pulls students into the setting and the story before we read, building interest while helping them visualize the history, while music adds another layer of immersion.

Never underestimate the power of music. Even one fitting song can add a subtle but unforgettable element to any lesson.

SPARK ENGAGEMENT

Music is at the heart of all the human cultures we study, but it's also in the heart of every child we teach. Playing music is one of the simplest and most powerful ways to pull students into the lesson and immerse them in the time or culture being studied.

When I'm feeling especially whimsical, I dim the lights and have students close their eyes.

"We're not in Hawai'i in 2026 today, class. We're in Philadelphia. It's the summer of 1787, and we're stepping into Independence Hall. The streets outside are alive with the clip-clop of horse hooves and the creak of carriage wheels (I hit two coconut shells together—Monty Python style). Inside, the air is thick and stifling. The windows are shut and locked to keep the debates inside secret, trapping the summer heat. And worse than the heat is the smell of the fifty men in wool suits, some of whom haven't had a proper bath in days. Wooden chairs scrape against the floor, quills scratch across parchment, and there, presiding over it all, sits General Washington—stoic and dignified at the front of the room. He calls the chamber to attention."

I pound my gavel on the desk and a couple students jump.

I continue. "Around you, the tension is real. This room—small, stuffy, and sweltering—is where the future of the United States is being debated, word by word. And today, in this classroom, I mean, Independence Hall, we get to see and read exactly what was decided as these men drafted the Constitution of the United States. You can open your eyes."

It's pretty silly, but most students appreciate it. Though high school students are desperate to grow up fast, they still have a bit of childhood wonder that I hope to provoke. And trust me, that levity will come in handy when you pass out texts that were written by Enlightenment scholars in the eighteenth century for them to analyze and annotate.

SPARK EXCITEMENT

Have the courage to be cheesy and an absolute, unabashed history nerd with your students. They might roll their eyes—but deep down, they love when teachers go all out. Embrace the cringe.

But even going all out to get students excited about reading a historical document will not be enough if they don't understand what primary sources are, why historians use them, and most importantly how to decode and understand them.

Intro Activity for Primary Sources: Historians from the Year 3240

My go-to anchor activity to introduce students to primary sources thrusts learners a thousand years into the future into an investigation I call Historians from the Year 3240. It's weird. It's fun. And students do a little archaeology and history while building skills they'll use to analyze primary sources throughout the year.

Students are placed in groups of four or five, and each student needs to provide one personal artifact: football, Stanley mug, makeup, class schedule, bus pass, Chromebook—whatever. Just make sure each artifact is different.

They are given this scenario: You and your group are historians from a future civilization, tasked with uncovering what life was like for teenagers in the United States in the year 2026. Your mission? Analyze a collection of mysterious artifacts discovered at an ancient school to piece together the story of teenage life in this time period.

These artifacts are your only clues—so pay close attention! Each one holds valuable information about teen culture, their responsibilities, technology, their interests, and the lives they lived. Your job is to carefully examine each artifact, discuss its possible meanings, and construct a detailed picture of what life was like for teens in 2026.

Work together, think critically, and let the artifacts guide you. What secrets of the past will you uncover? Get investigating!

SPARK ENGAGEMENT

Give students a role to play, and they'll lean into the learning. Whether they're detectives cracking a historical mystery, future historians uncovering the past, or forensic analysts piecing together clues from a crime scene, stepping into character makes a lesson an experience.

Students then complete the observation and inference sheet. Through the lens of history detectives, they realize how much can be uncovered from everyday objects.

This activity trains students to go beyond the obvious—to dig deeper and think critically. A bus pass isn't just a ticket to ride—it hints at mobility, infrastructure, economic status, and a student's daily grind. It sets the bar for the kind of thinking expected in class: thoughtful, analytical, and willing to ask, "What else could this tell us?"

HISTORIANS FROM THE YEAR 3240 PRIMARY SOURCE ANALYSIS SHEET

Name: Date:

SCENARIO: You are historians from the year 3240 trying to figure out what life was like in the United States for teenagers in the year 2026. You discovered seven artifacts and from only these primary sources you have to write a report on your conclusions about life for American teenagers in the year 2026.

INSTRUCTIONS

1. Each group member shares one or two personal items they have on them that will serve as an "artifact" and primary source until you have a total of seven artifacts.
2. The group will carefully analyze each "artifact" together—recording their observations and inferences.
3. After analyzing each one, you will write your interpretations report about life for American teenagers in the year 2026.

ARTIFACT	**OBSERVATIONS & DESCRIPTIONS**: Record details about what you see and what it is.	**INFERENCES** Record details about what this artifact can tell us about life in 2026 for teenagers.	**QUESTION(S)** What questions would this source likely give future historians?
1.			
2.			
3.			
4.			
5.			
6.			
7.			

FINAL REPORT: Using just your seven artifacts, write a report of your conclusions about what you, as a historian, can tell about life for teenagers in the year 2026.

REFLECTING: What did this activity teach you about primary sources and how or why historians use them to learn about the past?

After analyzing each source, students write up their conclusions. You could end it here or take it a step further by mixing up the groups and having them share their reports with their peers. Students will notice the differences in their conclusions based on the different objects they used. With such varying reports, students begin to understand that all primary sources have limitations—telling only part of the story. Scan the QR code to access this activity.

And once students understand what primary sources are, as well as why and how we use them, the next step is to get students to see beyond the document and understand the invisible historical forces impacting them.

SPARK CONFIDENCE

Nothing strengthens a classroom community more than students believing in themselves and each other. Even a "boring" lesson is meaningful when students leave with a sense of accomplishment and camaraderie.

Sourcing: Where the Dance Begins

Primary sources are already challenging for students to read and understand, but a bigger hurdle for them is recognizing there are many more forces at play than first meet the eye. All sources, primary and secondary, carry biases, but primary sources in particular are written or created from a particular point of view and can be misleading in ways that students must learn to detect and take into account.

To meet this challenge, students must learn how to think critically about what they read. If analyzing primary sources is "dancing with the dead," we want to make sure that our students take the lead rather than be led blindly into accepting the document's claims at face value. As history detectives in training, students must learn to approach all sources with healthy skepticism. And this begins with sourcing.

Sourcing helps us *see beyond the document* to assess its reliability and usefulness. Bruce Lesh teaches that it's essential to see documents in three dimensions rather than the two dimensions of the document itself. The invisible historical forces making up the other dimension include the historical context, the background and point of view of the author, the purpose of the document, and the audience. Teaching this three-dimensions metaphor will help students better internalize the importance of sourcing and looking beyond the text.

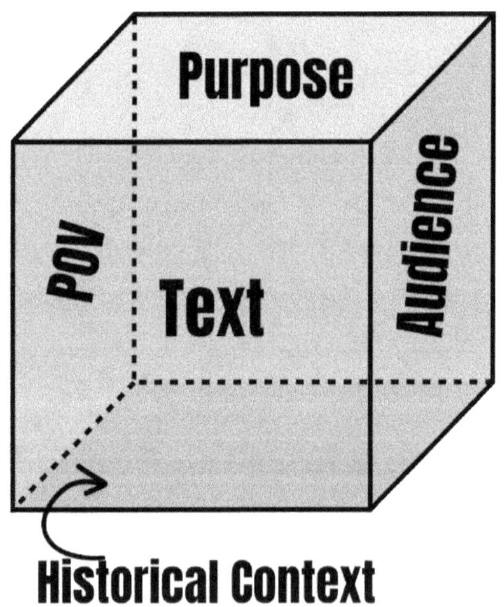

Can we truly grasp King's "I Have a Dream" speech if we don't put the speech into the context of the civil rights movement and consider why he delivered it on the steps of the Lincoln Memorial? Can students fully appreciate Hammurabi's code if they don't recognize this as an early civilization's attempt to impose legal order? Not a chance.

Sourcing is the first step to get students to think like historians. But let's be honest. Most students have as much interest in thinking like historians as they do thinking like librarians, accountants, or parking meter attendants.

To get students excited about sourcing, reframe this skill set. Sell it as thinking like detectives, investigators, or history hackers! History hackers and detectives read between the lines, gather clues and evidence, and uncover hidden truths that others don't notice.

SPARK CURIOSITY

Sometimes great teachers have to be great marketers. You can't just deliver the content; you have to sell it so students buy in and become invested in the learning.

Sourcing Strategies

Here are three common, no-prep strategies for sourcing documents. These are simple acronyms that task students with identifying and explaining each of the sourcing categories:

1. HIPPO: historical context, intended audience, purpose, point of view, and outside information
2. APPARTS (pronounced *AP parts*): author, place and time, prior knowledge, audience, reason, the main idea, significance
3. SCOAPS: speaker, critique, occasion, audience, purpose, subject

Most teachers will be more familiar with SOAPS, but I find that lacks one critical element for analyzing sources: critique. SCOAPS isn't just a better acronym than SOAPS (since it's a way to *scope* out the past); the critique element prods students to consider opposing positions and perspectives that were held at the time. This helps them recognize history was not just a single narrative—something that is often tricky for students to get their minds around.

Sourcing in general teaches students to enter a document with a more skeptical, investigative mindset. Adding the critique element doubles down on that habit. (Scan the QR code to access the template.)

For example, when analyzing Thomas Paine's *Common Sense*, students will better appreciate how radical an idea independence was if they use their background knowledge to recognize that loyalists and King George III were fundamentally opposed to his position. And this helps students get a more accurate understanding of the document and the history surrounding it.

By routinely sourcing documents, we aim to help students make document sourcing second nature—not just in our classrooms, but anytime they consume media and information.

SPARK EMPOWERMENT

Students will forget about 95 percent of the content you teach, but the skills stick. Students don't need to leave our courses knowing all the history, but if they become critical thinkers and passionate learners, we will have succeeded.

NAME: ______________________ Date: __________

SCOAPS

ANALYZING SOURCES TO EXPLORE HISTORY!

AUTHOR: ________________ TITLE: ______________________

DATE: ___________________ TYPE OF DOCUMENT: ____________________

Directions: Read or analyze the document carefully and fill in the boxes to analyze and source it!

S **SUBJECT** What is the topic or big idea of this document?	
C **Critique** Who at the time would critique this document? Why?	
O **OCCASION** What was happening "outside" this document that is relevant? What larger event(s) influenced it?	
A **AUDIENCE** Who is the intended audience? Who is the author trying to target or influence?	
P **PURPOSE** Why was this created? What does the author want the audience to do or think?	
S **SPEAKER** What do you know about the author? Include the background or point of view of the author.	
CONCLUSIONS What does this document reveal about the time period? What insights or new understandings does it give us?	

The Primary Source Sandwich

Hooking students into a primary source is one thing; keeping them engaged with sustained effort is another. With challenging texts, struggling learners might tap out right when they need to lock in. To help these students be successful, I created the Primary Source Sandwich.

It's delicious, it's nutritious, and it's jam-packed with skill development. Inspired by EduProtocols, this low-prep activity can be created quickly and used routinely. It pairs a juicy primary source text with two historical images related to the ideas in the text or to the inquiry question being explored.

PRIMARY SOURCE SANDWICH

PROMPT: How did the belief in Manifest Destiny impact America's development as a nation?

Document A: John Gast, "American Progress," 1872.

Document B: "Westward the Course of Empire Takes Its Way," by Emanuel Gottlieb Leutze, 1860.

Document C: John O'Sullivan, "The Great Nation of Futurity," The United States Democratic Review, 1839. *with modifications

Note: John O'Sullivan coined the term *Manifest Destiny*—that America had a God-given right to expand across the continent and spread its institutions and culture.

The American people having derived their origin from many other nations, and the Declaration of National Independence being entirely based on the great principle of human equality, these facts demonstrate at once our disconnected position to other nations. Our national birth was the beginning of a new history, the formation and progress of an untried political system, which separates us from the past and connects us with the future only.

It is so destined, because the principle upon which a nation is organized fixes its destiny, and that of equality is perfect, is universal. The far reaching, the boundless future will be the era of American greatness. America is destined to manifest to mankind the excellence of divine principles....Its floor shall be a hemisphere-its roof the firmament of the star-studded heavens, and its congregation a Union of many Republics, comprising hundreds of happy millions, calling, owning no man master, but governed by God's natural and moral law of equality, the law of brotherhood.

Yes, we are the nation of progress, of individual freedom, of universal enfranchisement (voting). Equality of rights is the heart of our union. We must onward to the fulfilment of our mission-to the entire development freedom of thought, freedom of person, freedom of trade and business pursuits, universality of freedom and equality. This is our high destiny, and in nature's eternal and we must accomplish it. [America's] high example shall smite unto death the tyranny of kings and tyrants, and carry peace and goodness to the world. Who, then, can doubt that our country is destined to be the great nation of futurity?

PROMPT: How did the belief in Manifest Destiny impact America's development as a nation?

Carefully analyze each source and then record details & reactions to them.

DETAILS	REACTION, QUESTION, OR INFERENCE
A	
B	
C	

Digging Deeper & Evaluating Sources	
What similarities do you see between all the sources?	Who in America at the time might challenge O'Sullivan's ideas?
According to O'Sullivan, what makes America that nation of the future?	How might the paintings in A and B be misleading? What are they leaving out or potentially misrepresenting?

Using evidence from the sources, answer the investigative question in a paragraph or two.

Essentially, the images are bait—hooking students into the topic by getting them curious. But they also help learners make connections to the text, which supports our struggling readers. You could use cartoons, propaganda posters, photographs, maps, or graphs—all of these will get students interested and prime them for text analysis.

On the back of the sheet are scaffolded questions that guide students through the analysis and sourcing process:

1. Observations, inferences, reactions, questions: Start with open-ended questions that allow students to pull details from each source that resonate with them.
2. Digging deeper: Take their thinking deeper with sourcing, corroborating evidence, and close reading questions that challenge students to compare the different sources and their evidence or arguments.

3. Investigative question: Bringing it all together, students write a brief argument to answer the prompt using evidence from the sources.

The Primary Source Sandwich is essentially a bite-size DBQ, or document-based question. But unlike a traditional DBQ, which can be daunting for students, the Primary Source Sandwich is approachable and helps students develop historical thinking skills incrementally. The multiple sources included in a Primary Source Sandwich help students begin to see history through multiple perspectives, revealing clashing viewpoints and competing narratives.

SPARK CONFIDENCE

Students need consistent practice to develop confidence in historical thinking. With it, they can make huge strides over a school year. Practice builds competence, and competence fuels confidence.

To truly engage students in history, we have to pull them beyond surface-level narratives into the deeper, more complex realities of the past. That's where the real beauty of history lies—in the messy, complicated web of conflicting narratives. In the hard truth of it.

But students, like most people, are desperate for a single, simple story with a clear moral lesson at the end—stamped with approval by all historians. A textbook and traditional lecture often offer just that—a single, polished, and digestible narrative. But primary sources reveal multiple perspectives, competing truths, and unresolved tensions. This makes historical documents challenging but also fascinating—if we can just get students comfortable working through the complexity. To appreciate the beauty in the messy reality of history takes time and practice.

SPARK EMPOWERMENT

The first sign of struggle triggers fear of failure for some students. That is why resilience and confidence matter—because everything worthwhile in education is found on the other end of productive struggle.

In *Why Learn History (When It's Already on Your Phone)*, Sam Wineburg argues that students need to develop "a muscle for ambiguity." The "unnatural act" of thinking like a historian requires students to get comfortable with historical uncertainty and to grapple with contradictions. So, take students out of their "single narrative comfort zone" gradually. Over time, with support and guidance, primary sources help students develop their muscle so they can sit comfortably with the ambiguity and uncertainty of history.

Because historical thinking isn't about memorizing what happened—it's about learning how to think through what *might have happened* and coming to informed conclusions about a past where the evidence doesn't always agree or add up.

And when students are ready to move beyond a few documents to full historical investigations, it's time to introduce them to the ultimate inquiry strategy—history labs.

5

HISTORY LABS

Get Students Doing History

I was greeting students at the door, dressed in a navy blue jumpsuit, sleeves rolled up, rocking a pair of work boots, with a red bandanna tied over my head. The *Pink Panther* theme blared from my speakers. Students shuffled in, some giggling at my outfit, but when they spotted the document stations and read the investigation question on the board "What happened to Rosie after the war?" you could feel them perk up.

They knew it was a history lab day.

Several students were already getting into character. Some were donning fake mustaches, others grabbed the novelty wooden pipes and magnifying glasses, and both the knockoff fedoras were being worn.

SPARK EXCITEMENT

Passion is contagious. By dressing up in costume for a lesson, students can't help but become more excited to learn.

It was the fourth quarter, so my students were veteran history detectives at this point. One of the benefits of using a handful of strategies routinely throughout the year is that I spend very little time reviewing instructions, expectations, and the skills students need to deploy during the activity. This leaves much more time for the good stuff: learning and sharpening skills. It also means students go into the activity confident they know what it takes to be successful. And when students feel comfortable with a task, it helps reluctant and struggling learners engage.

For this lesson, I only had to hook them and set the stage for the investigation. When the bell rang, I asked my class, "So, who am I dressed as today, students?"

"Rosie the Riveter!" several hollered.

"But definitely not as pretty," one student added.

"Or manly," chimed another as the class burst into laughter.

To be fair, they were both right.

Brushing aside my wounded pride, I said, "Exactly! And what do we remember about Rosie the Riveter? With your neighbor, share everything you can recall about Rosie and women's changing roles during the war. You have sixty seconds—go!" After their table discussions, we reviewed the big ideas: women stepping into new positions in the workforce, serving in the armed forces, leading patriotic households, and feeling empowered by their contributions to the war effort. And now for the tension to pull them into the investigation.

"Well, detectives, today you are going to be doing a history lab to discover what happened to Rosie *after* the war. When millions of men return from overseas, what's going to become of Rosie and women's roles in the country?"

Hands shot up. "Women are definitely going to be shoved back in the kitchen," one student predicted.

"Yeah, but Rosie is going to be pissed about it," chimed another. The class nodded.

"Solid predictions!" I then reviewed the expectations for the activity. "Now, it's time to see how accurate your hypotheses are and discover what *actually* happened! You will visit six stations, analyzing different kinds of documents—a graph, a political cartoon, a few primary source readings, and an oh-so-juicy Folgers Coffee commercial. Now, what do we do before we analyze or read any document?"

"Source it!" a few students called out.

"Exactly! And as history detectives, do we take everything a document states at face value and trust its every word?"

"Heck no!" students hollered.

"All right, detectives, you'll have seven minutes at each station. Sharpen your pencils, minds, and mustaches—you've got history to inspect!" Flexing my puny bicep, I told them, "We can do it!"

They rolled their eyes and jumped into the work.

For the next hour, students rotated through stations, piecing together evidence and discussing their findings. I popped in and out of groups, asking probing questions to stir deeper thinking. Then they went back to their desks and began corroborating and evaluating the evidence. The lab culminated the next class period with students creating a 1950s-style commercial that portrayed a more accurate depiction of women's roles in the postwar years.

And so went one of my favorite labs of the year. Students wrestled with history, made connections to modern-day gender roles, and completed a creative project that got them applying historical thinking skills in a memorable way. The fact that I got to lead this lesson dressed as an iconic symbol of Americana was icing on the cake.

What Is a History Lab?

Two people must be acknowledged for helping to develop and popularize the use of history labs: Sam Wineburg and Bruce Lesh.

You probably know Dr. Wineburg for starting the Stanford History Education Group, or SHEG, which recently rebranded as Digital

Inquiry Group (DIG). DIG offers a library of free curriculum and resources for history teachers—some that could be used for history labs and others that build the skills needed for them.

But my introduction to history labs came from Bruce Lesh. His book, *"Why Won't You Just Tell Us the Answer?": Teaching Historical Thinking in Grades 7–12*, is a must-read for any social studies teacher looking to start using labs and shift to inquiry-based learning with their classes.

When I attended Lesh's workshop, he led us through a history lab investigating whether President Theodore Roosevelt was responsible for orchestrating a coup in Panama to secure US control of the canal zone. It was 9:00 a.m. on a Saturday. A room full of history teachers, running on coffee and curiosity, were digging into documents like Teddy himself was on trial in front of us. We questioned motives. We debated perspectives. We tore into sources and scrutinized evidence. And by the end, Lesh had awoken the inner historian in every one of us.

I was hooked. This wasn't just learning history; this was living it. And I couldn't wait to bring that energy into my classroom.

Ditching the DBQ for History Labs

At first glance, it's easy to equate history labs with DBQs (document-based questions), or as I have heard my own AP students mutter, the "dreaded boring questions." While they share some similarities, labs and DBQs differ in a few critical ways.

Like DBQs, history labs require students to analyze a series of historical documents to answer a prompt. But here's the first key difference: In a lab, not all evidence is created equal. And that changes everything.

In a DBQ, students are generally on a hunting and gathering mission. They read the documents to collect evidence and then deposit that evidence in their essays to support their argument. They may be asked to source the documents in their prep work, but rarely are they pushed to scrutinize, critique, and even more importantly *discard* questionable evidence or sources.

Having graded thousands of AP US History DBQs at the College Board reading, I can attest that even the finest essays, surely written by some of the top student scholars in the country, reveal this. Scant few account for bias or consider the reliability of evidence. Almost always, students take the evidence at face value and use it to support their arguments. It's not the students' fault, nor is it their teachers'—certainly my students were doing the same. The structure of the DBQ simply doesn't encourage the habit of mind needed to consider these elements.

A speech by a politician, an amendment to the Constitution, a political cartoon, and a propaganda poster are all treated as equally valid sources. They aren't. And they require different degrees of scrutiny to determine their reliability and usefulness.

In history labs, students are encouraged to discriminate against documents and their evidence. "Does this cartoon really help me understand why Lincoln issued the Emancipation Proclamation, or is this merely reflecting someone's opinion? Why does this speech from Lincoln at Gettysburg differ from this one he delivered to religious leaders a year earlier? What do these differences reveal about his actual motivations?"

These are the kinds of questions we want students asking. Because if they develop these habits of mind in history class, they'll take them into the real world—where media literacy and critical thinking have never been more important.

And here's the other big difference between labs and DBQs: Labs prioritize the process as much as the product. Generally, the goal of the DBQ is to write an essay backed with historical evidence—which is great, don't get me wrong. But the goal of a history lab is that students seriously wrestle with documents and evidence before coming to their conclusions. The conclusions matter, but the struggle and process getting there matters as well.

In math, students show their work because the problem-solving process is just as valuable as the final answer. History labs operate the same way. They prioritize how students think through evidence—analyzing, questioning, and corroborating. It's not just about the conclusion they reach in the end. In the age of AI, this is more critically important than ever.

That's the real power of a history lab: Students don't just answer a question—they develop the critical thinking skills they'll need in the real world.

SPARK CONFIDENCE

A serious challenge can either crush a student's spirit or ignite it. They might not yet believe in their own abilities, but if you believe in them, they will start to rise to face those challenges.

History Labs and Twenty-First-Century Literacy Skills

Evidence is not enough anymore.

For decades it's been the gold standard in our classrooms: Create an argument. Support it with evidence.

Well, in a world where you can find evidence to support any claim, no matter how absurd, providing evidence will no longer suffice. One can now find "evidence" for aliens building the pyramids, Bigfoot stomping around the Pacific Northwest, or Hitler enjoying retirement in postwar Argentina. And these are just things you can learn on the History channel!

Even worse than the History channel are the social media platforms where the majority of our students get their information and ideas about the world. It's a media environment where the hottest takes get the most clicks, where everyone's an expert *and* a journalist, and where the hard and messy truth gets buried under a storm of propaganda, disinformation, and utter bullshit.

Voltaire warned that those who can get you to believe absurdities can get you to commit atrocities. Look around. We're living in a golden age of absurdities. All backed with *evidence.* Without skepticism, context, and literacy skills, the flimsiest of evidence can be convincing.

To prepare our students to navigate today's media landscape, we need to help them develop critical literacy skills. Because if our ultimate goal as history teachers is to develop informed citizens in a world awash in disinformation, our jobs have never been more challenging—nor more important!

And that's without even factoring in artificial intelligence, which is becoming a go-to search tool for many students and adults. Even when it's *not* hallucinating sources or inventing facts (which it does with alarming frequency), it tends to flatten the past—reducing rich, complex stories into oversimplified summaries that lack the prose and serious scholarship you can at least find in textbooks.

Even when AI is prompted for more complexity, there is a bigger issue: What is this response *based on*? What sources or perspectives were privileged in its coding? What bias is baked into its programming? How do we "source" AI?

Then there's the deepfakes, voice clones, and AI bots masquerading as people, spewing misinformation designed to deceive and sow discord. And greater challenges are coming down the pipeline.

So, no. Evidence is not enough anymore.

Students need both twenty-first-century literacy skills and the habits of mind to deploy them. They need finely tuned bullshit detectors and the skills to ruthlessly scrutinize evidence before accepting it. "Who is saying this? What agenda and expertise do they have? What's motivating their take on this issue? How does this evidence stack up to other arguments from reliable sources?"

But here's the good news. As history teachers, we are uniquely equipped to develop these literacy skills because we have a secret weapon: historical thinking skills. And while this has been a part of our pedagogy for decades, it's time we crank up the dial. Equal to the importance of developing historical knowledge must be the development of the skills needed to think critically about that knowledge. As Sam Wineburg puts it, students must become "problem-solvers of information."

Here's the even better news. We get to build these skills with a strategy that is engaging and bridges the gap between rigorous and fun. History labs turn learning history into a meaningful challenge—an investigation where students get to piece together a puzzle of the past and learn history by *doing* history.

SPARK CONFIDENCE

If you want students to take big risks in class, first get successful at tackling small ones together. Small victories, stacked over time, create a classroom culture where students can feel brave enough to be vulnerable, safe enough to fail, and bold enough to face any challenge.

The First Lab Should Be a Fun One

In fact, your first history lab shouldn't even be related to history at all. Kick things off with DIG's free Lunchroom Fight activity. In it, students play the role of a principal trying to determine what happened at a lunchroom fight based on the accounts of multiple people involved—the boys who fought, their parents, friends, eyewitnesses, and some adults on campus.

Students learn how to consider biases, context, and the reliability of sources in a fun anchor activity you can reference all year long. In the end, they have to fill out a suspension report based on their conclusions, which will lead to a lively debate.

Follow this up with a real history lab where students can put these skills to work. Make it challenging but not overwhelming so students enjoy their first real lab and see how exciting it can be to investigate the past.

SPARK CONFIDENCE

First impressions matter. When students are successful with a new strategy, they'll look forward to doing it again. Rack up early wins so you can ratchet up the rigor throughout the year.

How to Create Great History Labs

I hesitate to offer a step-by-step guide on creating history labs because there is no one way to do them. My labs look very different from how I was taught by Bruce Lesh. I took what I learned and modified it until the labs worked for me and my students. And I encourage you to do the same.

Therefore, take this as a guide, not a map. Find your own way and have fun doing it.

1. Start with a Compelling Question

The quality of the lab rests on the quality of the inquiry question. It's the engine that drives the whole investigation.

The question is really the lab's first hook. It should draw students in even before getting into the documents. While it's great if a question is provocative or controversial, what's most important is that it is clear. Fantastically and exceptionally clear. That means student friendly, so ditch the convoluted academic language of state standards or prompts that the College Board uses for its AP exams (unless you're preparing students for such exams, of course). A jargon-filled or confusing prompt will leave students wrestling with the question itself rather than with the history and documents. You want the heavy lifting to be in struggling over the sources, ideas, and evidence—not in trying to understand what the heck they're needing to answer to begin with.

Finally, the question should be grounded in understanding history, not an opinion. For example, "Should Truman have dropped the atomic bombs on Japan?" is provocative and interesting, but it can be answered with a knee-jerk "Hell no!" based on moral objections alone. Reframing it as "What convinced Truman that dropping the atomic bombs on Japan was justified?" is provocative while requiring students to contend with history to answer it. Debating the merits of his decision can come later.

2. Use Documents That Force Decision-Making

The best labs create tension. When students confront conflicting perspectives, they can't just collect evidence—they have to make decisions. Wrestling with contradictory sources forces them to examine not just the documents but the people and context behind them.

That tension is the puzzle. It's what makes labs compelling. So choose documents that will activate students' detective minds.

In one lab, my students tackled the question "Was America the land of the free during the time of Jacksonian democracy?" They examined a Frederick Douglass speech, an article from John O'Sullivan on Manifest Destiny, a voter turnout graph, a map, and the painting *American Progress.*

During our class discussion, Mahina paused and said, "I'm lost. Douglass's and O'Sullivan's arguments about America are totally opposite. It's like they were living in two totally different Americas!"

Bingo.

That realization cuts to the heart of history labs. Mahina's "two Americas" insight helped the whole class better understand that there is not just one history—because there is not just one present. Douglass and O'Sullivan certainly were living in two different Americas, and their conflicting perspectives help us develop a more complete understanding of America in the Jacksonian period.

Last, enrich the investigation with a range of document types: text, art, music, political cartoons, graphs, even short videos, if applicable.

3. Create an Atmosphere of Investigation

Set the tone *before* students walk in. A great history lab begins with a sense of anticipation and excitement.

Start with music. I swear by the *Pink Panther* theme, but any detective-ish or suspenseful soundtrack works. For our Triangle Shirtwaist Factory fire investigation, I use real fire truck audio from YouTube—sirens, engines, radio chatter—to transport students to the scene.

Donning a costume is totally optional, but it makes it more fun. Whether you're a detective, a CSI agent, or a historical figure, getting into character adds an unforgettable element to the lab. Sure, you'll get weird looks at the copy machine, but students will get interested the moment they see you.

Set up your room with stations, each featuring a single document. Use yellow "evidence" markers (like the ones from crime scenes, but miniature) to label them. This simple visual touch sets the mood, gives the lesson a natural flow, and helps students focus on one source at a time. I prefer having groups go station to station, but this setup works great for a jigsaw activity as well.

And don't underestimate the power of props and novelty "artifacts." If you want students to get into the detective spirit, fifty fake mustaches for five bucks on Amazon is money well spent, in my book. Some old fedoras, magnifying glasses, and Sherlock Holmes novelty pipes will get all but the "too cool for school" students excited for the detective work ahead. And if you can bring in any hands-on artifacts, all the better. Yes, genuine replicas would be great, but we're teachers on a budget, so get crafty.

For my Triangle Shirtwaist Factory fire lab, I burned old white linens at my house the night before and scattered the charred remnants around the room, leaving a smoky scent as another layer of immersion. A cigarette butt sat in a glass jar at the station, detailing the cause of the fire, and a white blouse hung nearby for a tactile connection to the lesson.

It doesn't need to be this elaborate to still have an impact. Here are some ideas for other labs:

- American Revolution: Brew Earl Grey tea, don a tricorn hat, and display a tarred and feathered cardboard loyalist.
- Ancient Egypt: Bring gauze strips for "mummification" and draw some hieroglyphics on "papyrus" made from a brown paper bag.
- Silk Road: Display spices and a silk scarf as trade goods.
- The Gold Rush: Scatter fake or fool's gold, display a mining pan and pick, create an aged and hand-drawn map, and hang a "Wanted" poster for an anonymous scoundrel who looks suspiciously like you.

Yes, these theatrical elements take time to prepare, but they're not just for your students—they're for you too! When you craft a lesson that's immersive, fun, and theatrical, you're reigniting your own passion for teaching. These labs don't just energize the students—they energize *you*! Because when you're excited to teach, students can feel it. And that shared enthusiasm? That's the magic that makes history unforgettable and teaching so wonderful.

4. Start with a Hypothesis

Just like a science lab, a history lab should begin with a hypothesis. Before diving into the documents, have students (either individually or in small groups) make an educated guess about the answer to the lab's central question. It gives them more ownership, and with their gears already turning, even the most challenging documents become more manageable.

5. Start Investigating

With few variations, I use the History Detective sheet for my history labs. On the front side, students source each document, gather relevant evidence, and assess its credibility and biases. At each station, they spend about seven minutes analyzing and discussing the document in groups while recording their insights.

But the real heavy lifting begins in the second part of the lab. After sourcing and gathering evidence, students transition to information problem-solving mode. Honing their historical thinking skills, they identify commonalities and contradictions, consider the usefulness of each document, and come to well-reasoned conclusions to answer the inquiry question.

NAME: DATE:

HISTORY DETECTIVE SHEET

INVESTIGATION QUESTION	

What do I already know about this topic?	HYPOTHESIZE: What is your initial guess or prediction?

SOURCING Record details about the source.	RELIABILITY What makes this source reliable? What makes it potentially unreliable or biased?	USEFUL DETAILS & EVIDENCE Gather important details that can help answer the inquiry question.

What differences do you notice between the sources and different accounts?	What similarities do you notice? What conclusions or generalizations can you make with confidence?

Which document do you think is most reliable or helpful to answer this question? Why?	Which document do you think is least reliable or helpful to answer this question? Why?

What questions do you still have or what information would better help you answer this?	What is a source that could help you get that information (secondary or primary)?

CONCLUSION: Answer the prompt starting with your thesis and then support it with evidence from the documents. Try to reference at least two documents in your response.

6. Hold a Mini Seminar

Before students move on to a final assessment, open the floor for a discussion. An informal discussion or mini seminar allows students to hear from each other, consider differing ideas, pose new questions, and reflect on the challenges they faced. Sometimes, this is the most worthwhile part of the whole lab.

> **SPARK CONFIDENCE**
>
> **Asking students to reflect on and share the challenges they faced normalizes the fact that learning is sometimes tough and frustrating. It shows them that struggling is not just normal—it's beneficial.**

7. Complete an Assessment

Unlike a DBQ, which culminates in an essay, a history lab can conclude in a variety of ways. It could end with a formal seminar, a short written response, a mock trial, group presentations, a creative project, or, yes, a document-based essay.

Students need ample opportunities to write because it's a powerful tool for processing the challenging ideas they confront in history class, but it's not the only way they can demonstrate their thinking.

Whatever the assessment, it should challenge students to grapple with the documents, hone their critical thinking skills, and in the process, deepen their understanding of history. If students walk away feeling more confident and enjoying the process, that's the greatest win of all.

Three of My Favorite History Labs

Confederate Monuments

As the final project for my Civil War unit, students act as an executive committee on Confederate monuments. Their task is to analyze primary and secondary sources to develop a workable, real-world solution for what should be done with Confederate monuments in the United States.

The documents guide them through key questions: Why were these monuments erected in the first place? What messages and values do they convey? And, from watching recent news clips, what are public attitudes toward them today? Instead of just creating an argument about whether the monuments should stay or go, students do the more meaningful work of proposing a policy to address the issue.

After they have developed their solution, students take it a step further and design a new monument that commemorates the Civil War and the values we seek to uphold as Americans today. They create a mock-up design, explain its symbolism, and write an inscription for it. And then they present all of this to the class: the policy solution and their monument design.

This lab hits everything I love about teaching history. It gets students wrestling with historical documents, engaging with a pressing issue impacting us today, building problem-solving skills, and expressing their ideas with a creative and artistic challenge.

Ultimately, I hope it helps students understand that we do not just inherit history—we shape it.

What Happened to Rosie?

My second-favorite lab, detailed at the start of this chapter, gets students exploring women's roles after World War II. They analyze documents to piece together the complex realities of gender roles in the postwar era.

The lab culminates in a creative challenge. Students perform their own commercial for a product from the 1950s or 1960s. Their ads must either reflect the perspective of one of the documents or present a more accurate depiction of gender norms and women's roles at the time.

Shihuangdi and the First Book Burning

With only three documents, this is a perfect primer lab that I use early in the year for my freshman World History class. I set the stage with traditional Chinese music, scatter burnt scraps of old newspapers, and put police tape and "Do Not Read" signs on my bookcases. (To be fair, some of my students are usually thrilled with this new classroom policy.)

The documents include a secondary source, a Qin official's decree announcing which books were to be confiscated and punishments for noncompliance, and a painting of a book burning created three centuries later that also shows the burying alive of Confucian scholars. These sources provide just enough depth and complexity for students to wrestle with arguments and evidence without feeling overwhelmed early in the year.

It's a little lab that leads to big ideas. Students explore censorship, governmental authority, and efforts to erase history. It brings to life the old adage that "knowledge is power." Hearing students argue about the importance of history and why history must be preserved is music to my ears.

The lab concludes with a Venn diagram comparing the Qin dynasty's book burning with banned books in US history. I close the lab with these words: "If history wasn't important, tyrants wouldn't try to erase it. And when they try, it's up to us to preserve it."

A Revolution in History Education

History labs aren't just another teaching strategy; they're a revolution in how we engage students in the study of the past and prepare them for the future. Lab-style inquiry helps them learn history while developing civic literacy at a time of misinformation, polarization, and rising threats to democracy.

So, no, this won't be easy. And no, the old ways won't suffice.

But we can't let fear or uncertainty hold us back. We ask our students to take risks every day—to struggle through challenges, speak up, and get back up each time they fall. We owe it to them to do the same. To model courage. To try something new and dare to fail forward.

It's a challenge that I hope excites you and pulls out your best teacher self. This isn't a "take your medicine" moment. This is a challenge worthy of our efforts, talents, and passions. It's why we became teachers to begin with: because we believe in the promise of education and the hope of a better tomorrow.

We can do this. We *get* to do this!

6

HISTORY DECISION SIMULATIONS

It's usually not best practice to lie to students or rewrite history—but for this lesson, I couldn't resist.

Before the lie, though, students were locked in a high-stakes simulation figuring out how to save the world from nuclear oblivion. As they stepped into class, they were given role cards: President John F. Kennedy, Secretary of Defense Robert McNamara, Secretary of State Dean Rusk, and Attorney General Robert Kennedy.

Before revealing the U2 spy photographs of Soviet missile sites in Cuba, I called all the President Kennedys forward. Placing their left hand on our textbook and right hand in the air, the presidents took the oath of office: "I do solemnly swear that I will faithfully execute the Office of President of the United States, and will to the best of my ability, preserve, protect and defend the Constitution of the United States."

Some snickered when they were told to take the oath. They always do. But after, most of them took on a certain authority and gravitas.

SPARK ENGAGEMENT

When putting students into historical roles, the smallest gesture can help them get into character. A simple prop, an oath of office, role cards with official titles, or name tags can get students to lean into their roles and take the work more seriously.

Then came the folders—manila envelopes stamped with "TOP SECRET" containing all the intel students needed. Inside they found mock presidential briefings, real U2 photos of Soviet missile sites, maps, and a timeline.

Then, I briefed them: "The president has assembled you—the Executive Committee of the National Security Council (ExComm)—to help him navigate the most consequential decision in human history: How should the United States respond to the discovery of Soviet nuclear missile sites in Cuba? There is no map. No guidebook. No precedent you can look to. The fate of humanity and the eyes of history are on you. Good luck. The clock is ticking."

With my brief lecture, my goal is not just to set the stage for the activity but to raise the stakes so students feel the weight of the moment. History gets dusty and dull when it's just facts and bullet points. But history is high drama. Pressure. Decisions. To make that tension come alive, we need to bring that energy front and center in our lessons.

After my briefing, ExComm groups dug into their documents, reading, annotating, and debating how to solve the crisis. Five options lay before them:

1. Ignore the missiles.
2. Launch a full invasion of Cuba.
3. Enact an air strike on missile sites.
4. Engage in a naval blockade of Cuba.
5. Send a diplomat to meet with the Soviets.

To make an informed decision, students had to seriously grapple with history. They had to consider Cold War concepts like the containment policy, the Truman Doctrine, the arms race, and Kennedy's blunder with the Bay of Pigs.

More than that, students were emotionally engaged with what stood in the balance. How could they avoid nuclear war while still projecting strength and resolve? You know the simulation is working when a student states to his group, "Do you want the blood of millions on your hands? Come on!"

After coming to their decisions, each group's President Kennedy went to the front of the room, donned my blue blazer with the American flag lapel pin, and delivered their speech to the American people announcing and justifying their decision. I tracked the results on the board:

- Ignoring the missiles = 0
- Full invasion = 1
- Air strikes on missile sites = 1
- Naval blockade = 2
- Diplomacy = 3

After delivering their speeches, students were dying to know what Kennedy actually did, and they had no idea I was about to pull a fast one on them.

SPARK ENGAGEMENT

A little "good stress" goes a long way. If students feel the pressure to "get it right," it means they're invested in the content and the outcome. It means they care enough to take it seriously.

Bringing up my slideshow, I announced, "For thirteen tense days, the Executive Committee of the National Security Council debated behind closed doors. Some pushed for an airstrike, others for diplomacy. In the end, President Kennedy decided . . . *drum roll, please* . . . What JFK decided to do in this dark hour was . . . with the fate of the humanity hanging in the balance . . ."

"Gosh! What did he do, Mr. Lewer!"

It's not often that students are at the edge of their seats, desperate to learn a historical fact. Can you blame me for relishing the moment?

"In the end, President Kennedy decided . . . to ignore the missiles!"

Stunned silence. Students stared at me and the words *Ignored the missiles* on my PowerPoint in utter confusion. It soon turned to outrage.

"No way!"

"Wait! That doesn't make any sense."

"That's the worst decision he could have made! It doesn't project strength or protect America's national security." I stood there relishing in their bewilderment.

Then, I clicked to the next slide: *JUST JOKING* with a laughing SpongeBob GIF. There were some chuckles but mostly boos and head shaking. It was the reaction I wanted. Their confusion and anger showed me they cared about the history and learned enough to realize something didn't add up.

I then taught them what actually happened. The naval blockade, the standoff, Khrushchev blinking, the hotline, etc. Though most groups had come to a different decision, the process opened the door for students to critically evaluate Kennedy's actions.

And they left the lesson having learned a heck of a lot more than just what happened during the Cuban Missile Crisis. They left understanding *how* history is made and *why* careful decision-making matters—and, hopefully, they're more ready to *act* on the daunting problems we face today.

That is the power of history decision simulations.

It's what led me to make this a central pillar of my curriculum. Because when students are thrown into a moment of historical crisis, forced to make the call—something changes. History stops being *back then* and starts feeling like *right now*.

SPARK EMPOWERMENT

Asking students for their opinions or challenging them to develop their own solutions to historical problems makes history more personal and relevant. It gives them a voice in class and a stake in the content.

Why Use Historical Decision Simulations?

Every history teacher has asked their students this classic question: "What would *you* have done in this situation?"

Maybe it was during your Ötzi the Iceman lesson, asking students how they would have tried to survive if they were injured and stranded in the Alps. Or maybe you were projecting Dorothea Lange's famous *Migrant Mother* photograph and asking students what they would be thinking if they were her or the children.

That simple shift—inviting students into the moment—changes how they see history. It sparks empathy. It triggers curiosity. And it spurs critical thinking. Because when students imagine themselves in the content, the stakes change. It's not about remembering what someone else did—it's about considering what *they* might do.

The question I always struggled with, though, was how to take this further.

How do we move past quick, surface-level reactions and create experiences where students truly inhabit the moment? How do we thrust them into a real historical dilemma where the next move actually matters—where they have to wrestle with tough choices, conflicting values, and the real risk of failure and catastrophe?

The answer, I realized, is simple: Zoom into the conflict. The richer the conflict, the richer the experience. And lucky for us, history is packed to the brim with high-stakes conflicts, power struggles, and moral dilemmas. Our job is to stop skimming past those moments and instead zoom in, slow down, and teach history more from the first-person point of view.

SPARK EMPOWERMENT

History hits differently when students stop asking, "What did they do?" and start asking, "What would *I* do?"

Slow Down and Zoom In

The US history textbook on my classroom shelves covers the topic of prewar appeasement in three paragraphs. My world history textbook devotes almost a half page to it. It goes something like this: Hitler rebuilds the German military in violation of the Treaty of Versailles. Nazi troops march into the Rhineland. Britain and France, still reeling from the Depression and traumatized by World War I, wag their fingers. Hitler, sensing weakness, annexes Austria, then the Sudetenland, then all of Czechoslovakia. The emboldened Nazis then blitzkrieg into Poland. Finally, Britain and France declare war. World War II begins.

That's the ten-thousand-foot view at ten thousand miles per hour. Students might remember a few bullet points for a few days. But if we want them to understand why appeasement failed and why it matters today, we need to slow the lesson down and double-click into the conflict and tension.

Because appeasement isn't only essential to understand World War II. It's the prequel to Cold War containment. And it still shapes how nations respond to threats today. So, I wanted this lesson to stick. I wanted students to see how appeasement unraveled one step at a time. I wanted students to sense how each decision to act was an opportunity to impact history. And how deciding not to act carries its own consequences.

So I planned a decision simulation.

Students were placed in groups of four: two British leaders, two French in each group. Briefing sheets placed them in the mindset of their countries—war-weary, economically fragile, politically unstable. Then, over five escalating scenarios, students had to decide how to respond to fascist aggression. In brief, here are the scenarios I used:

1. Scenario 1: It's 1935 and Italy has invaded Ethiopia. Violating the Treaty of Versailles, Hitler rebuilds Germany's military. Students debate, deliberate, and then announce their decision to the class. Most issue firm warnings but no action. (I tracked their decisions on the board and then revealed what really happened.)
2. Scenario 2: It's 1936 and Hitler moves troops into the Rhineland. (Some groups called for economic sanctions, a few started rearming, but most held back.)
3. Scenario 3: 1938. Austria is annexed. (Now students were growing wary. They began issuing stronger threats, some calling for trade embargoes, others continuing to build up their militaries.)
4. Scenario 4: Later in 1938, Hitler is now demanding the Sudetenland, a German-speaking region of Czechoslovakia. (Some students now drew the line and called for war, some threatened a blockade, but a few still clung to compromise. When I read Chamberlain's infamous "Peace for Our Time" statement, students laughed at the bitter irony. I announced how within a month, Hitler took the rest of Czechoslovakia.)

5. Scenario 5: It's 1939 and Nazi forces invade Poland. (There was no more debate. Every group declared war. History had caught up with them.)

With every passing round, students grew more engaged, frustrated, and surprisingly hardened by the geopolitical realities of the simulation. The tension built as fascist aggression became more emboldened in front of them. The challenges of war and peace were not just covered in the abstract; they came to life at their table debates and in their decisions.

We closed with a reflective discussion: "What is the essential lesson we must learn from this episode to create a better future?" Some students made it personal: "You can't ignore a problem and hope it goes away. You need to face it." Others pulled global lessons about nations standing up to threats, even if it meant war.

Decision simulations like this transform abstract concepts into emotional, ethical, and intellectual experiences. When you slow down and place students in the center of historical events, they're much more likely to retain the content and the underlying importance far beyond the unit test.

Interesting Problems to Solve

"Give students interesting problems to solve."

That is the advice to teachers from marketing guru and best-selling author Seth Godin. To prepare students for the demands of the twenty-first century and to build leadership skills, Godin says that students need to be given complex problems to grapple with.

Trying to prevent a nuclear holocaust and responding to fascist aggression are, in my book, interesting problems to solve. So is figuring out how India could gain independence from the British empire without using violence. Or what governing philosophy would be best to manage the newly unified state under the Qin dynasty. Or how to secure workers' rights during the Gilded Age, when unions were illegal and the government had management's back. All these topics would thus make great history decision simulations.

Which would your students remember more—being told how Gandhi gained independence for India or trying to develop a plan to achieve that themselves? Which would engage them more—reading an overview on the foundations of Legalism or acting as Shihuangdi's advisers, debating and deciding the most effective system of government for China? Which would best prepare your students for citizenship—a worksheet on the Pullman Strike or acting as Eugene Debs and union leaders to strategize how to secure better conditions for industrial workers?

This is not a cutting-edge idea. Problem-based learning goes back decades. Its place in history education, though, could be better utilized and prioritized. Grappling with the conflicts and problems at critical moments in the past is a powerful way for students to learn history while developing the skills and instincts for civic engagement.

SPARK EMPOWERMENT

Don't steal the struggle by coming to the rescue. Let students sit with the challenge and fight their way through. That's where growth happens. That's when students truly own their learning.

History decision simulations flip the script on how history is traditionally taught. Instead of looking at history through the clean lens of hindsight, students experience it in the heat of the moment. Without the benefit of hindsight, students feel the weight of the historical moment pressing down. With only the documents to guide them, students must consider competing priorities and grapple with a mess of facts. This is where things truly get interesting—stepping into the unknown.

That tension of not knowing the outcome builds emotional investment. And the act of making a decision gives students a powerful sense of agency. No longer just passive learners, they become active participants. They're the changemakers—the man or woman in the arena.

In Defense of (Some) Boring Lessons

Sorry to interrupt, but I need to get something off my chest before going any further.

As much as I believe students deserve dynamic, meaningful, and exciting learning opportunities, they also need simple, routine, and, yes, sometimes even boring ones.

Though this book is dedicated to strategies that make history engaging, there is nothing wrong with an ordinary lesson.

It took me years to appreciate this, but sometimes engagement is quiet. Sometimes what students need most is a quiet space to read, write, and think. In fact, some students prefer these simple moments and learn best when given individual time to work on note-taking, reading comprehension, or completing a worksheet. A snapshot of this lesson won't get many clicks on Instagram, but that doesn't mean it isn't great teaching.

When I was a new teacher, I believed it was a cardinal sin to use the textbook, and I drove myself nearly to exhaustion trying to plan new and exciting activities every day. I grew uncomfortable and anxious if my classroom was quiet, even as students were locked in and diligently working. If that silence stretched for more than a few minutes, I felt the need to jump in to "get students engaged."

I was chasing the theater of engagement rather than what truly matters: student learning.

Great teaching is about balance. Just as students need time to talk, move, and have fun, they also need time to think deeply, struggle, and work through challenges on their own. Sometimes learning is joyous and exhilarating, and sometimes it can be frustrating or even a little boring. That is okay.

What great teachers do more than anything is ensure that day after day, students are learning.

Keep your eye on the prize.

How to Set Up History Decision Simulations

Like nearly all the strategies in this book, there's no single formula for a history decision simulation. Great teachers experiment with new strategies until they make them work for their students. I switch these up depending on the topic and the pacing needs of the unit. But there are key elements that make these simulations powerful, memorable, and worth the time it takes to slow down and zoom in.

No Spoilers

Let's start with what *not* to include: the ending! The suspense is everything, so don't spoil it or even hint at what actually happened in the end. It's the uncertainty that makes the activity interesting, so you want to build up the suspense and then release students to navigate the problem on their own.

Sometimes, though, you have some budding history buffs in class who already know what happened. Give them a special role: the provocateur! Their task? Stir the pot, push back on the group consensus, and make peers work for their decision. They'll relish the authority, and this will deepen the group's discussion.

On top of that, you will no doubt have students looking to google their way to the "right answer" and shortcut the whole activity. Here's the thing you want to tell them: "There is no right answer. Some historical choices were wrong, or it's still debated if they were the right call. Better options could have been taken. The point here isn't to just learn what happened. It's to feel the weight of this moment in history—just like the historical figures you're acting as did. So don't cheat yourself out of the challenge. Don't skip the struggle. That's where the growth is. That's where the story becomes yours. And don't worry! I'll teach you what really happened after you all come to your own decisions on how history should have been written."

Appeal to their better nature. You might be surprised how many step up when they feel the work matters.

Characters Brought to Life

To care about the crisis, students need to understand the people at the center of it. If they're acting as Napoleon, they must know and care about him. Bring this character to life for your students with a quick video bio or story lecture, or let the briefing documents themselves breathe life into key figures.

Narrative and Context

Students need to understand the world they're stepping into. Start with a briefing document—a text that lays out the crisis through a story-based narrative while providing essential content needed to understand the event. I also like to include images, primary source quotes, maps (if relevant), and a timeline.

My briefings are normally one and a half to three pages for a simulation that can be completed in two class periods or about ninety minutes.

Tension

If you want students to care, *really* care, about a historical decision, you've got to make them feel the weight of it. That starts with you. Your direct instruction should do more than just review the facts and set the context. It should breathe life into the moment, stirring up drama, urgency, and a sense of duty.

For students to appreciate the importance of the decision, ratchet up the tension and keep the conflict at the center. Too often, students dismiss critical moments in history with a shrug because they're so distant from them: "Oh, hundreds of women protested outside the White House, were arrested, beaten, and force-fed while demanding the right to vote? *Yawn.*" "A bunch of powdered-wig-wearing men in 1776 were debating how to build a republic from scratch? *Snooze fest.*"

To combat this emotional disengagement, you want to create good stress. Not the kind that overwhelms but the kind that electrifies. It's that emotional jolt when students actually care about what they're doing and feel that the work really matters.

Decision-Making Sheets

Students aren't used to solving national security threats or organizing independence movements (kids these days, right?). So they need support. That's where a decision-making sheet comes in handy. You want the sheet to scaffold their thinking: understanding the context, recognizing limitations of the power, weighing their options, thinking strategically, anticipating likely outcomes and what might backfire. The point is to slow them down to force deeper reflection and more careful decision-making.

NAME ____________________ DATE ____________________

Presidential Decisions in History

CONTEXT: Summarize the issue at hand in a few sentences.

Who are the key groups involved or interested in this issue?	LIMITATIONS: What practical or constitutional limitations constrain your ability to handle this?

UNDERSTANDING YOUR OPTIONS List different choices you have to solve this dilemma. Obvious & outside the box.	DESIRED OUTCOME If all goes perfectly, what would you like the outcome to be?

DECISION: Make your initial decision. Be clear and specific with your plan in 2–3 sentences.

Presidential Decisions in History

ANTICIPATING UNINTENDED CONSEQUENCES: What is something that could go wrong or backfire?	MAKING ADJUSTMENTS: Can you do anything to limit that risk?

WINNING HEARTS & MINDS: How can you "sell" your decision to voters and the American people to win their approval and support?

Write out your speech announcing your decision to the American people. Include important details on how you came to this decision and what the expected outcomes will be.

SPARK EXCITEMENT

When students are fired up for a challenge, it feels like adventure, not frustration. That's when you can really raise the bar, and they'll rise to meet it.

Final Assessment

There are plenty of ways to end these activities. You could do a Socratic-style seminar discussing the dilemma and students' decisions, maybe poster boards detailing their decisions. But I prefer to have students write speeches—especially if they're acting as the president or another leader. Their speeches review the crisis, defend their decision, and lay out the results they're anticipating, all while trying to win over and reassure their audience.

Make sure to set up class so their speeches are worthy of the moment. All students should be facing forward. The podium should be front and center. If a student is acting as president, a blue blazer with an American flag lapel pin will give them some presidential swagger, and a prop microphone is a nice touch as well. If the audience is moved, a standing ovation may be in order.

Make sure to track student decisions on the board to build more suspense before the big reveal.

Closure: Teaching What Actually Happened

At this point, students should be desperate to know how the actual history played out. I generally lead a brief lecture reviewing the decision, the effects, and why it matters.

Make sure to allow time for students to reflect and discuss their thoughts on the actual decision. After seeing how it played out, do they agree that it was the best way to handle it? Or do they think another option would have been better? This helps students recognize that history was not set in stone and that it was shaped by real people making tough decisions in times of actual crisis. The goal is not just to help students learn the history but to learn *from* history so they can improve their own decision-making and problem-solving skills. The goal is that they walk away empowered. A reflective discussion helps with that.

Into the Arena

This framework can be adapted to nearly any historical topic. Your students could act as John Smith, scrambling to save the floundering Jamestown colony before it collapses. Or Gail Halvorsen, figuring out how to drop candy from the sky to the children of Berlin without disrupting the airlift. Or they're members of the White Rose, risking everything to spread anti-Nazi leaflets while avoiding the watchful eye of the Gestapo.

Make it your own. Toss out what doesn't work or steal my framework wholesale with the QR code. But bring your own flair and own passions to the mix. One teacher on social media gave these decision simulations a Dungeons & Dragons twist to teach trench warfare. Students took on different roles and used twenty-sided dice to face skills challenges, react to real-time developments, and navigate random battlefield events. *How cool!*

Beyond academic growth, these simulations train students for something much bigger: civic action.

Because democracy cannot run on autopilot. We need to develop citizens who can act and care enough to do so. Democracy requires people who can think carefully, consider different perspectives, and take action, especially when it feels daunting. These simulations cut through the double-edged sword of apathy and paralysis that many young people feel when considering the challenges we face today. By giving students agency and a framework to work through complex challenges, we help them improve their problem-solving and leadership skills.

Every time they step into a historical figure's shoes, every time they stare down a crisis, every time they make a decision or map out a plan of action, they build the muscle and instinct for civic engagement. It reminds them that history was shaped by people who chose to act—people not unlike themselves. And hopefully, it helps them become citizens who don't just sit back and wait for change but instead have the courage, wisdom, and nerve to fight for the world they want to create.

7

FOSTERING DEEP STUDENT-LED DISCUSSIONS

Two weeks into my semester-long cross-country sabbatical, I stepped into one of the most prestigious high schools not just in New York City but in the country—and felt every bit the outsider. Not just because I was rocking a bright aloha shirt on a frigid January morning. Teaching at a small, rural Title I school in Hawai'i, in a classroom that is nearing a century old (and it shows), I was overwhelmed by the grandness of the place. Twelve stories, towering New Deal–style murals, a school theater that moonlights as an off-Broadway venue, a hall of fame boasting generals, Olympians, and CEOs. I felt I was in for something special.

After observing a STEM class building towers out of marshmallow and spaghetti, I raced down the marble hallways during the passing period looking for room 318. I was set to observe an English teacher—let's call him Mr. Davis. Sliding in just before the bell, I grabbed a seat in the back of the room and opened my notebook to record my observations. Sixty minutes and five pages of notes later, I jotted down, "This is teaching and learning at its absolute finest."

My sabbatical had just begun, and I'd found the gold I was searching for.

Over the next five months, I would visit over sixty schools: public, private, charter, magnet, religious, inner-city, rural—you name it. One day I would be passing through metal detectors and armed guards at the doors, and the next I'd be at a school that had an open-locker policy where lockers were left physically open to foster greater trust on campus. Criss-crossing the country on a teacher's budget, I couch-surfed, crashed in spare rooms, and camped in national parks along the way. I was on a mission to discover the best teaching practices from the best practitioners. I've always believed the surest way to grow as an educator is to see pedagogy in action—to see how great teachers put theory into practice.

I saw a lot of incredible and cutting-edge stuff. Escape-room activities where students cracked codes by solving puzzles to unlock new challenges. Mini museum exhibits, virtual field trips with 3D goggles, and the makings of a student-produced film festival. But what hit me the most—over and over again—wasn't flashy, techy, or cutting-edge at all. It was something ancient and mundane, just done incredibly well.

It was students talking and making meaning together. And no one did it better than Mr. Davis. After the sixty minutes in his room, I knew exactly why I went on this sabbatical and what I hoped to bring back to my own practice and classroom.

When the bell rang, Mr. Davis announced to the class, "Please form the discussion circles. Remember, if you are not in the inner circle today, you will have to be for the next discussion." Students reassembled the desks from pods into an inner circle and outer circle, and grabbed their readings and notebooks. Mr. Davis, sitting at his desk, well removed from the discussion area, leaned back in his chair and asked who would like to facilitate the discussion. A young man raised his hand.

"Great. Michael, open it up with a question."

From there, the discussion took off. No one raised their hands. No one interrupted or talked over each other. They cited the text, questioned assumptions, built off each other's ideas, and made real-world connections while Michael pulled in his peers to ensure everyone had opportunities to share. Occasionally, Mr. Davis asked the outer circle to share their notes to summarize the conversation—but otherwise, he said nothing. This went on for nearly thirty minutes without a single awkward silence.

To close class, students completed a reflection sheet breaking down what they learned and how they performed in the discussion. This, I realized, is a crucial but often ignored step to help students make strides with their discussion skills. Sure, this was an AP English class at a prestigious high school. But what happened in that classroom wasn't magic or preordained. It was a result of a class culture built on curiosity combined with high expectations and the guidance that got them there. Practiced and polished until students didn't just participate in the seminar; they owned it.

When I returned to my own classroom, we never reached the level of discourse I witnessed in room 318. But that experience gave me a target to aim for. And little by little, our discussions grew deeper. Students started listening more, thinking deeper, sharing more confidently, and, best of all, looking forward to circling up together. And I'll count that as a win. How I brought that kind of discussion culture into my own classroom, and how you can, too, is the focus of this chapter.

Importance of Academic Discussion in History Classrooms

There's a huge push in education to make learning more hands-on. And I get it—students want to build, move, experiment, and create. Though I love a good hands-on project, what is most exciting and worthwhile for history is a heads-on endeavor. It's about wrestling with big ideas, confronting the uncomfortable, thinking through controversies, and developing the courage to take a public stand. And discussions give students the opportunity to do that with their peers in real time.

Even when discussions fall short, they're still worth it. Because they're real. They can't be faked, copied from a neighbor's paper, or spit out by AI. They are a window into what students know, what they're wondering, and what they're stuck on or confused about. It gives all students a voice and the space to share it. In that way, they are not just human; they're democratic.

Thomas Jefferson said that New England's town hall meetings were "the best school of political liberty the world ever saw." And today, that town hall begins in our classrooms. An open discussion with peers is democracy in action, a cradle for liberty and self-government.

In a circle, no one is above anyone else. Everyone gets a voice. And in the process, students learn how to share ideas, disagree respectfully, and challenge ideas without tearing each other down. They get to listen. They get to hear diverse ideas and new perspectives. And this is a skill and norm the world, and our country in particular, desperately needs now.

Let's face it—the world outside the classroom doesn't exactly model healthy discourse. It's a dumpster fire. A fever dream of shouting matches, vulgarity, and hyperbole. The public square has been replaced by social media echo chambers that reward provocation over understanding, hot takes over humility, and conspiracies over the boring, messy truth. Why participate in a respectful discussion when you can *own* and *destroy* your opponents? Why listen respectfully and curiously when shouting gets the clicks and the likes?

If students don't learn how to engage in healthy discussions in our classrooms, they'll learn it from Reddit threads, YouTube comments, and the open sewer of an X feed.

In a media landscape that rewards discord, boasting, and owning others, we need to develop students and future citizens who can reflect quietly, think openly, and speak civilly. That's why discussions aren't a *nice-to-have* in social studies classes. They're essential.

And to make discussions work, every student has to feel safe enough to speak and respected enough to be heard. They need the confidence to share and the humility to listen. That starts long before you circle up and start the seminar.

Discussions Start with Community

Fostering rich academic discussions doesn't start with content. It starts with community. It starts with trust.

Students can't engage in real (which often means vulnerable) dialogue unless they feel safe. That's why we spend time at the start of the year building community through icebreakers, team-building activities, and low-stakes collaboration. That's why we make space for silliness—because fun builds the kind of relationships that make taking real academic risks possible. Shy kids won't raise their hand to share an idea, especially one they're unsure about, if they worry a wrong answer will be mocked or an unpopular opinion ridiculed. And forget about lively whole-class discussions if students aren't willing to ask questions aloud or if they don't feel safe pushing back against each other's ideas.

Ironically, for students to feel safe enough to think independently, they need a community that values it. It requires a classroom culture that respects differences and celebrates the oddball insight, the quirky question, and the outside-the-box answer.

SPARK COMMUNITY

Nothing breaks down barriers and builds bridges like laughter. Classes that have fun together can be pushed to do hard things together.

So, step 1 for class discussions is to create a culture where students feel seen, safe, and supported—not just by you but by their peers. Community building, thus, doesn't end after the first week of school. Keep nurturing connection and culture all year long. Take quick routine breaks from the grind to do fun activities that mix it up and build camaraderie. Even a silly ten-minute game can make a big difference in how students interact, trust, and open up with one another. A little joy goes a long way.

Building Skills and Confidence

After community, step 2 is practice. And lots of it. Informal discussions are the best training ground for more formal seminars.

Every lesson should include opportunities for students to discuss ideas with one another. Daily practice with listening and speaking to peers has a compounding effect over the course of the year. That's why my bell work routine goes from individual work to pair-shares to whole-group discussions—every single day. It's why I break up readings, lectures, and worksheets with short wiki-chats where students share their understanding, opinions, or questions.

There are two skills we need to coach students on to support rich discussions: active listening and speaking up with confidence.

Discussions are an act of public speaking, and for many students, public speaking is terrifying. For teenagers already racked with anxiety, there's something about sitting in a circle and sharing ideas that feels like a spotlight aimed directly at their insecurities. It's natural for some to shut down under that pressure.

Some of the brightest students in class might also be the most quiet and shy ones. They may be unstoppable with pen and paper or behind a Chromebook screen, but when it comes to participation in a discussion, they shrink or disappear completely. But to have great discussions, you need—the class needs—their voices amplified.

So coach your students, especially the shy ones, when you work one-on-one or in small groups with them. Get them to believe their voice is worth sharing and applaud them when they do.

SPARK EMPOWERMENT

When a student shares a great answer, resist repeating it to the class yourself—instead, put it back on the student. "Bravely, share that great idea again, but louder, please, so we all benefit from hearing it again."

Encouraging Bold and Wild Ideas

The infamous street artist Banksy said, "Think outside the box, collapse the box, and take a f**king sharp knife to it." That is not just sound advice for rebellious artists—it's a philosophy for classrooms that want students to think for themselves.

Because we don't need more parrots echoing back what they think the teacher wants to hear. That happens on its own. We need students brave enough to share ideas that might be wrong or weird but maybe also brilliant, or at least worth considering. And that takes cultivating.

On my sabbatical, I saw that the classrooms with the most meaningful discussions weren't filled with students chasing the "right answer." They were filled with students who felt safe enough to share original thoughts, make wild connections, and question the obvious. Not hot takes for attention's sake—but ideas that made their classmates think in new ways.

So, how do we get there?

For starters, you cannot simply tell students that mistakes are okay in your classroom. You cannot just put up a cute poster that reads "Mistakes are how we learn!" You need to encourage and celebrate brave and unique ideas. Ask your class, "Who has a really creative and interesting wrong answer to question four?" When Michelle shares a totally unhinged response, address the inaccuracy but praise her creative thinking. When Carlos makes a totally bizarre connection that other students scoff at, run over and slap him five or have the whole class celebrate him with two claps and a snap. Make it a moment.

When students feel safe enough to be wrong, they can dare to be great.

SPARK EMPOWERMENT

The goal of education is not striving toward perfection. It's striving to spark joy in learning, and nurturing an adventurous spirit of free thinking.

The Importance of Student Questions

Once students feel safe and confident enough to share ideas, the next thing they need to develop is the ability to ask great questions. And to do that, they first need to get in a lot of reps asking really bad ones.

While coming up with questions might be natural for kindergartners, it can feel like pulling teeth with secondary students. Somewhere between finger painting and freshman year, the average student has had their sense of wonder beaten out of them and pulverized into quiet compliance. In too many classrooms, students have stopped thinking for themselves and started waiting to be told what to do and think by the teacher. From a world of magical exploration, school becomes a daily grind. A to-do list of chores assigned by teachers. A diploma, for some students, is an accomplishment reduced to "time served."

Having students ask their own questions will not solve all these problems, but it's one small thing that, if prioritized, can have a massive impact. In *Make Just One Change: Teach Students to Ask Their Own Questions*, Dan Rothstein and Luz Santana argue that one of the most impactful ways to increase engagement and ownership is to let student questions guide the lesson. Imagine that.

When you make this change, expect resistance. When you first start asking students to come up with their own questions, you'll get a lot of this:

- "But what if I don't have any questions?"
- "What question *should* I ask?"
- "Is *this* a good question?"
- "Isn't another question just more work?"

These are not signs of laziness but of conditioning. Students have been in the passenger seat for so long that it's no wonder they struggle to drive their own learning. Curiosity is a mindset and a skill. Without practice and encouragement, it atrophies.

But here's the good news: If students start asking their own questions, the rest will follow. The discussion takes care of itself. Curiosity fuels the lesson. The class transforms. The learner owns the learning.

Little by little, the practice of asking questions rekindles students' sense of wonder while increasing the intrinsic motivation to learn. Instead of "Answer this question" or "Complete this task," it's "What do you wonder about this topic?" This creates an opportunity for students to think for themselves and confront their own interests and curiosities along the way. Because thinking for oneself begins with questioning for oneself.

SPARK EMPOWERMENT

Imagine this: Instead of students walking into class and asking you, "What do we have to do today?" now they're thinking, *What will I choose to explore today?*

Strategies to Help Students Ask Great Questions

One of the most effective tools for getting students to ask questions is the Question Formulation Technique (QFT) from *Make Just One Change*. The basic idea is simple: Have students generate their own questions before diving into a topic.

But knowing students' natural hesitation and worries about asking the "right questions," Rothstein and Santana recommend these guidelines to combat that resistance.

Spark Interest

Start with a short teaser or bit of context—just enough to hook them. "We're starting a unit on the Neolithic Revolution, when humans first discovered agriculture and the practice of farming. In your groups, generate as many questions as you can about this in the next five minutes."

Ask Away

These three guidelines will help get the questions flowing:

1. No judgment: Do not worry about the quality of the questions. Just record as many as possible.
2. As is: Write down questions exactly as stated. Don't worry about editing or improving them.
3. Statements to questions: If it sounds like a statement, flip it into a question.

Sort and Flip

Next, students sort their questions into two buckets:

1. Closed: These are simple, factual answers.
2. Open: These are complex answers that require explanation.

Then to practice asking different types of questions and to help them see how changing a few words can totally transform a question, students flip a few by turning closed into open questions and vice versa.

Reflect and Share

Have students pick a couple of their favorite questions to share with the class. This forces them to reflect on what makes a question worth asking and allows them to hear other questions from their peers.

Three Levels of Questions

While I love the QFT, I tweak it a little to also include Dr. Arthur L. Costa's Three Levels of Questioning. Instead of just open and closed, Costa's Three Levels add an additional layer that ensures a discussion covers the essential content, fosters critical thinking, and deepens the analysis by making connections beyond the text or topic itself. Here are the levels.

1. **LEVEL 1—IN THE TEXT:** This can point to the answer in the text. For example, "How many pigs were in the story? What did the second little pig use to build his house?"
2. **LEVEL 2—IN BETWEEN THE LINES:** Students must read between the lines and analyze information to answer. For example, "Which pig was the most intelligent? What is the moral of the story?"
3. **LEVEL 3—BEYOND THE TEXT:** This cannot be answered by the text itself. It connects the themes and ideas to things beyond the text. For example, "Who is the wolf that children need to be prepared for today? Are parents and schools preparing kids for the challenges of the real world?"

Intro Activities to Help Students Learn to Ask Great Questions

How do you put those strategies into action? As always before diving into serious content, start with something familiar or fun to help students build their questioning muscle.

For years, I kicked this off with story time using a classic fairy tale. I'd shove the desks aside, have students sit on their notebooks in a circle, and read *The Three Little Pigs*. It might sound childish, but it generally led to a deep discussion and got students enjoying the process of formulating questions.

SPARK EMPOWERMENT

Student questions are the cornerstone of a student-centered classroom. To really own their learning, students must be empowered to explore their curiosities.

Music works great too. I've used Johnny Cash's "A Boy Named Sue," and we listen and read the lyrics together. It's a catchy song that tells a story full of action and irony, with a sentimental twist at the end that gets kids thinking about bullying, gender roles, parenting, and what it takes to make it in the world today. For the rest of their lives, if they ever hear that song, they'll think of your class and that lesson.

Art is another great entry point. Any painting that tells a story or is dripping with symbolism should spark students' interest. Pablo Picasso's *Guernica* leads to a deluge of questions during my "rise of dictators" lesson, for example. But maybe the best hook I've ever used to get students questioning was in my introduction to Hinduism. I projected an image of the god Ganesha and let the questions roll: "Why does he (she?) have an elephant head?" "Why four arms?" "What does the flower represent?" "What is Ganesha the god of?" "Why is one tusk broken?"

In a few minutes, we had over a dozen unique questions. Then students spent ten minutes researching to answer as many of their questions as they could. In the process, they learned some of the basics of Hinduism and a ton of little factoids about Ganesha. But more importantly, their interest was piqued, they improved their questioning skills, and they were hungry to learn more. And that's the point.

SPARK EXCITEMENT

Curiosity is just interest looking for understanding. When students are intrigued, the questions and the desire to answer them come naturally.

When students start to ask their own questions, they take the wheel to drive their own learning. Any lesson can then be turned into an investigation and discussion. And while formal seminars and debates might be the gold standard, informal small-group discussions can also be powerful and are the best training ground for higher-stakes seminars.

Informal Activities to Engage Discussion

Discussions can feel abstract—floating in the ether. That makes it tough for some students to follow them, and even tougher for them to jump in and contribute. Hexagonal thinking gives conversations structure and shape (literally). It adds a tactile, hands-on layer that can help students engage in academic discourse.

This strategy works especially well for units packed with vocabulary, concepts, and key figures or as an end-of-quarter review. Put students in small groups with a set of fifteen to twenty-five paper hexagons, each labeled with a term from the unit. Their task is to build a honeycomb linking related terms edge to edge while discussing and debating their connections together. Every placement of a hexagonal term requires justification.

It's an open puzzle, a brainstorm, and a discussion all at once. It requires content knowledge, evidence, and argumentation. And the puzzle aspect of assembling it adds an element of fun.

To add structure and accountability, have students write short justifications for their connections—either on a worksheet or directly on their desks with Expo markers (a crowd favorite in my classroom). To deepen the learning, challenge them to label the various categories in their honeycombs.

If you're collecting these for a grade, students can glue their terms down on paper or snap a picture and upload it to a shared Google Slides presentation. For me, I grade these based on participation and engagement. If students were contributing and trying, it's A's across the board.

SPARK CONFIDENCE

Want students to believe that mistakes are part of the learning process? Then stop grading every formative task for accuracy. Grade for effort, not perfection—and save the red pen for the summative work, where it belongs.

Continuum Discussions

In my early years of teaching, when my discussions either fizzled out after a couple of minutes or spiraled off into gossip, there was one strategy that always seemed to work: continuum discussions.

Originally developed by History Alive! (now Teachers' Curriculum Institute, or TCI), this is another strategy that uses manipulatives (placards) to stir the discussion and prompt deeper thinking. Print out a series of placards, each with an image and a term that can be ranked against each other on a continuum.

For a lesson on the Enlightenment, I cut out placards with names and portraits of the following thinkers: John Locke, Voltaire, Rousseau, Montesquieu, and Mary Wollstonecraft. Students created a continuum with "Extremely Dangerous" on one end and "Hardly Dangerous" on the other. I gave them this scenario: "You're an absolute monarch, and there are Enlightenment thinkers running around your country spreading their revolutionary ideas. Rank the thinkers by how threatening their ideas are to your regime." Discussion groups had eight minutes to rank these thinkers on their continuums. Physically moving the placards across the continuum helped stir the debates and decision-making as students worked out their thoughts regarding the ideas that each thinker advocated.

To avoid groupthink or coming to a quick consensus, include these three parameters:

1. **START SOLO.** Have students rank the cards individually first by listing them out in their notebooks in order. This gives everyone an opinion to bring into the discussion.
2. **USE THE 3D RULE.** Discuss, debate, and only then decide.
3. **ADD TIME REQUIREMENTS.** If groups finish early, require them to justify their rankings in writing. Most groups prefer to talk, so this encourages deeper discussions.

Once groups finalize their rankings, launch a whole-class showdown. Print out large versions of each placard and invite one group to put their continuum in order on the front board and justify it to the class. Then open the floor to challengers for a whole-class debate. After their table discussions, students will be fired up and ready to defend their positions.

Bonus Rounds: Repeat with New Scenarios

Things get really fun when you switch up the scenarios for table discussions. Using the same placards you used for scenario 1, provide a new lens so students can take what they know and think about it in a whole new way.

- Scenario 2: "You're revolutionary leaders who just overthrew the French government! You are writing a new constitution for France and want to create the best government possible. Rank the Enlightenment thinkers by how important their ideas will be for writing your new constitution." (Continuum: "Most Important" to "Least Important.")
- Scenario 3: "You're students in a world history class in the year 2026 (crazy to consider, right?) debating the influence of Enlightenment thinkers on today's society. Considering the current state of the world, whose ideas have been most realized and whose ideas have not been fully realized?" (Continuum: "Most Realized" to "Least Realized.")

Same placards. Different lenses. Whole new insights. By providing different scenarios for the same terms, students can have more engaging, layered, and spicy conversations. As their mastery grows, so does their interest—by the third round, sit back and let them cook.

SPARK EMPOWERMENT

Competence begets confidence. Even the most reluctant learners begin to take pride in themselves when they can think deeply, speak clearly, and hold their own in a discussion.

Chat Stations

So you have students who like to run their mouths as well as their legs? Let them exercise both with chat stations.

Post four to seven thought-provoking questions around the room. In small groups, students rotate from station to station, spending a few minutes discussing each question. Recording their thinking is optional, but if you want receipts, you can have them do one of the following:

- Drop a hot take on a Post-it and leave it at the station.
- Jot down a quick summary on a shared group sheet.
- Write directly on butcher paper posted at each station using color-coded markers.

After visiting each station, circle up to debrief as a class.

Socratic Speed Dating

This strategy blends two powerful formats: Socratic seminars and speed dating.

If you've never done a normal speed dating activity, you're missing out. Any unit packed with colorful personalities is perfect for it—the Renaissance, French Revolution, antebellum era, or the 1960s. Each student takes on a historical figure, researches them, and then role-plays as that person. Require a prop or a costume piece as a delightful bonus. Then set up the room with desks in two rows facing each other, cue some romantic background music, dim the lights or drop in some battery-powered candles, and let the speed dating begin.

After a couple of minutes introducing themselves and discussing pressing matters of the day with each other, students rotate to the next desk. In the end, they form partnerships or "love triangles" based on shared goals or ideals. It's a great activity and especially fitting (and cringey) for Valentine's Day.

Socratic speed dating strips away the costumes and the partner-seeking aspect but keeps the rapid-fire exchanges. Set your room up with pairs of students facing each other—seated or standing. Project a discussion prompt and give them one to two minutes to dig in. Start simple: basic review, quick recall. Then escalate to deeper questions—opinions, ethical dilemmas, real-world connections.

It's a high-energy, structured strategy to get every student speaking, listening, and thinking, without the pressure of speaking in front of the whole class.

Best of all is that these informal, low-stakes discussion activities build real skills and confidence. With routine practice, students will be ready to engage in more formal academic discourse—seminars and debates.

Fiery Debates

Debates are a hallmark of a healthy democracy and thus should be a hallmark of a social studies education. They help students examine multiple perspectives on complex issues and give them the chance to take a stand, defend a position, and learn how to advocate for their beliefs while staying open to others.

Way more than other discussion activities, debates can get heated. This makes them exciting but potentially problematic. It's easy for a clash of ideas to take a slight turn into a clash of personalities and egos. I've had plenty of debates get derailed just as they were getting good because a kid jumped out of his chair and hollered, "Ooohhh!" after an emphatic point was landed by his side. Laughter erupts, and the discussion loses its momentum.

That's why norms are essential. You want to channel that energy into productive discourse. Though it's always a good idea to create these with your students' input, here are some basic norms that work well:

- Argue with ideas, not people.
- One voice at a time: If you're not sharing, you should be listening, thinking, or taking notes.

- Win with respect and dignity. Winning the debate is great, but the real goal is to sharpen your thinking and build bridges, not burn them.

Four-Corners Debates

After learning about President Hoover's response to the Great Depression, it's easy for students to believe he was a coldhearted jerk who didn't give a fig about the suffering of everyday Americans. To push their thinking deeper, we did a series of quick four-corners debates. Students gathered in the middle of the room, and I flashed a statement on the board. I asked students to migrate to the corner of the room that matched their stance: strongly agree, somewhat agree, somewhat disagree, or strongly disagree.

Here are the prompts we used:

- "President Hoover's approach to addressing the Great Depression was not just ineffective; it was cruel."
- "The government is responsible for helping people who are in poverty."
- "If people receive support from the government, they will be less motivated to help themselves."
- "The more powerful a government gets, the more corrupt it becomes."

Students had a moment to think, then moved to their corner. There, they huddled and shared their ideas together before jumping into a brief whole-class debate.

The most powerful moment came at the end. We revisited the first question, and nearly every student had shifted their stance. At the start, most believed Hoover's actions were cruel. By the end, although most still believed his response was ineffective, far fewer felt he acted out of malice. I hadn't taught them anything new. All that happened was students listened to each other's ideas and opinions and reconsidered their own.

SPARK EMPOWERMENT

As teachers, we are in the special position to not just "be the change we want to see in the world" but to make our classrooms the change we want to see in the world.

Philosophical Chairs

Philosophical Chairs is an AVID strategy that adds a little twist to traditional debates. After you pose a provocative prompt like "The printing press changed the world more than the internet" or "The civil rights movement accomplished its goals," students divide into three camps: support, oppose, and undecided.

After having time to prepare their arguments, the support and oppose sides go back and forth. The undecided or neutral students play a crucial role in asking clarifying questions and summarizing the most compelling arguments, and they can be swayed to a side mid-debate if they are won over.

Best of all, the undecided group votes on the winner. That means you don't have to play judge, jury, and referee. Students own the process.

Immersive Debates

One of the simplest ways to make debates more impassioned is to give students roles and drop them into the past. Don't just debate if the colonists should have declared independence; divide them between patriots and loyalists and have them duke it out like it's 1776. You can split students into the two sides, or better yet, assign individual historical figures to get them fully into character. And yeah, it would take a long time to create twenty-odd role cards for your students, but you could also find a lesson plan online, even if it costs a few bucks.

Of course, not every debate needs costumes and characters. When the goal is to help students develop their own opinions and wrestle with ideas, a traditional debate is more fitting. And when the goal isn't persuasion but exploration, a seminar is the call.

Socratic Seminars

A Socratic seminar is an open discussion where students explore ideas together. Unlike debates, which focus on persuasion and trying to win, seminars prioritize curiosity, collaboration, and meaning-making. Using the Socratic method of questioning and pushing back against assumptions and ideas, seminars offer students the chance to think deeply together in real time.

If debates are a destination with a map, seminars are somewhat of a maze. There's no road map, no finish line—just the journey itself. Your period three and seven seminars might look totally different, and that unpredictability is what makes seminars both challenging and meaningful. Embracing the challenge and uncertainty as a class is essential.

Set Up for a Seminar

The physical setup of the room matters. Rearrange seats into a single large circle or use the inner-outer circle for a fishbowl method (more on that later). The goal is simple: Everyone can see each other, and no one (including you) is in the spotlight. The form follows the function: having a democratic discussion.

Start small. Your first few seminars should be short and have low stakes—fifteen to twenty minutes is plenty. Early on, you'll need to model what a good seminar looks and sounds like. As the facilitator, here's what you need to do:

- **SET THE TONE.** Be calm, curious, and inclusive. "Let's open by exploring what King's dream really was. Who's ready to start us off?"
- **PUSH DEEPER.** "Ghenea, you said King's dream aligns with the American dream—can you say more?"
- **DEMAND EVIDENCE.** "Chance, what made you say King sees segregation as just one part of a larger problem? Can you tie that to the text?"
- **INVITE DIVERSE PERSPECTIVES.** "So far everyone's been in agreement on King's approach. Does anyone see it differently?"
- **REFOCUS WHEN NEEDED.** "We've shifted from Napu's point about the Declaration of Independence to voting rights to Malcolm X's ideas. Let's come back to the founding ideals and focus on that for a bit. Amy, would you like to chime in on that?"

As the facilitator, you also want to model interfering as little as possible. Let the discussion take form and grow on its own and only chime in when needed.

From Socratic Seminar to Harkness Discussions

By modeling how to facilitate the discussion, you're trying to put yourself out of a job. At some point, a student will take your seat. Seminars become truly empowering when students are not just participating but leading the discussion. That's when you've got yourself a Harkness discussion.

A Harkness discussion is similar to a Socratic seminar, except it's entirely student driven. The teacher sets up the discussion and then hands it over to the students to own the meaning-making process. To remove yourself from the discussion, it's important to physically remove yourself from the circle. When a Harkness discussion is firing on all cylinders, the teacher does little more than record the process, track participation, and occasionally pause to review or get the discussion back on track. Just like what I saw in Mr. Davis's classroom.

And when students are running the discussion, it's essential you resist your teacher's instinct to jump in, support, clarify, and correct. You're not the sage on the stage, nor the guide on the side. In a Harkness discussion, you're a fly on the wall. So buzz off and let the kids own the learning. (This is something I still struggle with, so this is also directed at the author.)

It might get messy. Awkward silences might stretch uncomfortably long. That's okay. Sit back and let the kids own it because that's part of the learning process. They need to know that the teacher is not coming to the rescue. You want students thinking, *Someone has got to get this conversation rolling. Why not me?*

SPARK EMPOWERMENT

Real empowerment happens when students stop looking to their teachers for support and confirmation and start looking to each other and themselves.

Fishbowl Discussions

Another way to structure a seminar is with a fishbowl setup: two concentric circles, with only the inner circle actively discussing while the outer circle observes and tracks the conversation. Fishbowls ease the pressure by narrowing the spotlight. Rather than thirty students all trying to jump in, there are only a handful "onstage" at once. This makes participation more manageable, especially for shy students and those who need more time to process.

Fishbowl discussions also provide built-in opportunities for reflection and feedback. After the discussion, students in the outer circle can share what they noticed—applauding contributions and offering tips for improvement. If outer-circle students tracked a specific peer, they can pair up afterward for a quick debrief.

The Hot Seat

To crank up the energy just a bit, add a hot seat. Leave a single open seat in the inner circle to allow for quick participation from the outer circle. Any student in the outer ring who feels struck by a question or insight can quietly step into the hot seat, share their idea, and then return to their seat in the outer circle. That one question or insight might kick-start a quiet or dwindling conversation.

Setting Up Great Seminars: Key Ingredients

1. **SET NORMS.** Keep them simple and review them regularly.
2. **PICK A PROVOCATIVE TEXT OR TWO:** Choose a juicy reading full of tension, conflict, or a moral dilemma. Use sources with differing perspectives or arguments as you would for a history lab.
3. **USE A DISCUSSION SHEET.** Provide students with a simple guide to organize their thoughts and prepare their questions.
4. **PREPARE WITH READING GROUPS.** Let students annotate, process, and practice discussing the text in small groups first.
5. **SET A PERSONAL GOAL:** Have students write a quick intention on their discussion sheet. This might look like "I'll contribute three times" or "I'll cite text evidence each time I share."
6. **ENGAGE IN POST-DISCUSSION REFLECTION.** After the discussion, allow time for students to consider what they learned, how they performed, and how they can improve.

WILSON & WWI SOCRATIC SEMINAR

INVESTIGATIVE QUESTION: Did President Wilson and the United States enter World War I to genuinely "make the world safe for democracy"?

DOCUMENT A

Author: Type of Document: Audience:

Purpose of Document:

JUICY QUOTE/PHRASE:	
2 "Ahas" or Important Details	2 Questions About This Document

This document shows Wilson (was or was not) being genuine to keep the world "safe for democracy" because

DOCUMENT B

Author: Type of Document: Audience:

Purpose of Document:

JUICY QUOTE/PHRASE:	
2 "Ahas" or Important Details	2 Questions About This Document

This document shows Wilson (was or was not) being genuine to keep the world "safe for democracy" because

SPARK EMPOWERMENT

Students are much more likely to meet goals they set rather than ones teachers tell them to work toward. When they set the goal, they own the process and the outcome.

The reflection might be the single most important part of this process to help students make progress and growth. As John Dewey stated, "We do not learn from experience. We learn from reflecting on experience."

Troubleshooting Common Problems with Seminars and Discussions

Sometimes, though, you do everything right and you're still left with crickets. Or maybe it's a three-student echo chamber. Or just as troublesome, everyone's talking, but no one's listening—the conversation jumps from one topic to the next without exploring any of them.

It happens. What is most important is not to get frustrated or disappointed. Students will feel that, and it will only heighten the angst and tension moving forward.

Respond instead with empathy or even humor. "Well, that was an epic fail. Let's give it another go. Civil Rights Movement seminar—take two! Lights, camera, discussion!"

Or you can try one of these responses to the four most common problems.

PROBLEM: There are lots of awkward silences and minimal participation.
THE FIX:

- Let the silence breathe. See if students will break it themselves.
- Try a turn-and-talk moment for one to two minutes, then reopen the circle.
- Jump in and narrow the focus—"Let's zero in on Malcolm X's belief in Black Nationalism. Who has a question or comment about that?"

PROBLEM: The same few students dominate the discussion.
THE FIX:

- Two cents rule—only two contributions per topic or question per student.
- "Three before me"—after speaking, wait for three others before contributing again.
- Award points for inviting others in. Provide these sentence stems for students: "Does anyone else think that [statement]?" "I'd love to hear someone share what they think about [topic]."

PROBLEM: There's lots of talking but no real discussion (Note: This often occurs when students know they're being graded for participation. They're hungry to share but struggling to build on ideas and actually converse.)
THE FIX:

- Act as or appoint a facilitator who can redirect. "Let's come back to Sophia's point and focus on that for a minute . . ."
- Award points for building on others' ideas or staying on topic, not just random participation.
- State the topics. You can state the focus and after five minutes, or when the conversation stalls, state the next topic. (This could also be when the inner and outer circle switch.)

PROBLEM: Students only talk to the teacher, not each other.
THE FIX:

- Before starting, remind them, "You're discussing this with one another, not with me."
- When they do talk to you, look down to your notes.
- Use neutral affirmations. Instead of providing commentary or praise, just say, "Thanks."
- Physically remove yourself from the circle and appoint a facilitator.

And if all of these fail, pull out the ace up your sleeve—the Socratic Smackdown.

Socratic Smackdown

Imagine a gamified and competitive seminar that rewards points based on quality participation and active engagement. That is what the Socratic Smackdown offers, as well as a chance for a group of students to be pronounced the "Seminar Champions of the Age of Imperialism"—or whatever topic you're exploring.

Developed by the Institute of Play in New York City, the Socratic Smackdown was designed to boost engagement and help students level up their discussion skills by adding fun and competition into the mix.

Here's how it works:

- Students are divided into teams of four to six and prepare for the seminar by reading, annotating, and generating questions.
- One team at a time has the inner circle for a timed discussion.
- Everyone in the circle is on the same team. The goal is not to defeat each other but to model an ideal, collaborative discussion and earn more points than other groups.
- Points are awarded for things like asking level-three questions, citing text evidence, disagreeing respectfully, and building on ideas. (Start with the basics and build from there.)

- The outer circle takes notes or tracks points based on a rubric. (Scan the QR code to access the free rubric provided by the Institute of Play.)
- In the end, the team with the most points wins.

To make it more exciting, lean into the gamification: Let teams choose names and hype songs and enter the circle like debate gladiators. Play their entrance music, flash a five-minute timer, and then let the dialogue begin.

Is that a silly way to start a Socratic seminar? Sure. But if the energy gets students engaged, so long as they get serious once the timer starts, the theatrics are worth it.

And while Socratic Smackdowns can make discussions more fun and memorable, especially for reluctant learners, the gold standard is still the traditional seminar or Harkness discussion. The points, music, and hype are a bridge, not the destination. The true power of a discussion shouldn't be in the competition but in the conversation and collaboration. It's the struggle to understand something complex, to wrestle with history, and to grow through conversation that matters most. The opportunity to think deeply about ideas worth struggling over is the ultimate reward.

Students will start to feel that when they're having great seminars, and I hope you feel ready to get them there.

8

ACTIVITIES AND PROJECTS THAT MAKE HISTORY STICK

While the rest of this book focuses on building strong routines as the foundation of a student-centered classroom, this chapter does something a little different.

This is where you'll find some of my favorite creative projects and activities from over the years.

Because routine lessons are essential. They are the solid foundation that helps students feel comfortable and confident enough to make major strides over time. But just as important as that structure is the occasional one-off activity to inject excitement into a unit.

In the book *The Tao of Teaching*, author Greta Nagel put it this way: "Without routine there is no learning. Without surprise, there is no wisdom."

This chapter is about that surprise—that impromptu activity to complete your unit.

Some of these are one-period tasks, and others are bigger projects that can anchor a unit. What they all share is their ability to get students engaged while building content knowledge, sharpening critical thinking, and, often, fostering creativity along the way.

Let's start with the basics before moving into more creative and complex projects.

Timelines

Timelines are cornerstones in history classes. They help students develop chronological reasoning, understand change over time, and break down the content into a mind map to see how history developed. Here are some fun ones you can use throughout the year.

Illustrated Timelines

Take a traditional timeline and mix in some art and visuals to help students think creatively and deeply. For each event on the timeline, students include a date, title, and brief summary plus an image, symbol, or quick sketch. Simple, fun, and effective.

POV Timelines

Point-of-view timelines help students develop historical empathy by showing the different ways various groups experienced the same events. Start with a standard timeline with a date and title, but have students describe how two different groups experienced or viewed each event. Some good POV timeline options would be tracking the road to Pearl Harbor, the causes of the American Revolution, or the origins of the Cold War.

Matching Review Timelines

This one is a high-energy, hands-on review game. Select five to ten events from the unit. For each event, print a date, event title, brief description, and image. Cut them up separately and scramble them, then drop all the pieces into a plastic bag. Repeat this for however many groups of students you have playing. Hand each group a bag, set a timer, and have students work to match and sequence them correctly on their desks. Make it a race to see which group can get them matched and in order first. After all groups finish (or the timer runs out), mix up the teams, shuffle the pieces, and go again. Students will master these events in no time while getting a chance to work with many of their peers. If they're high-fiving and calling for a rematch, it's working.

"Eras Tour" T-Shirt Designs

Look out, Swifties! This activity is inspired by an anonymous teacher who shared it in the comment section of one of my blogs. Students design a concert-style T-shirt for a historical era. On the front is a creative graphic and/or slogan that captures the spirit of the era. On the back are major events listed like tour dates—with the time and place of each event and some relevant images to decorate. Finish with a gallery walk and a class vote for best tour tee.

Sidewalk Chalk Mega Timelines

This is a great activity for the last few weeks of school, when the weather is warm and motivation is waning. Head out with some sidewalk chalk and have students create a mega timeline on the blacktop reviewing everything they learned this year. Take some pictures. Make some memories. It's a great way to end the year and a fun way to review before finals.

Creative Writing Tasks

While students need ample practice writing standard summaries and five-paragraph essays, providing opportunities for more creative and meaningful writing is just as essential. When I started offering more interesting writing tasks, I saw students put in more effort, enjoy the process, and even look forward to sharing their work with peers. This section includes creative writing prompts and tasks that can be used for nearly any topic or unit.

Investigative News Stories and Exposés

What better way than an exposé to conclude an investigative inquiry into controversial topics like the explosion of the USS *Maine*, child labor in the Industrial Revolution, or King Leopold's genocidal policies in the Congo? Students act as muckrakers, writing news stories exposing what they've discovered.

Here are the guidelines:

- Include at least three of the five senses: what you saw, felt, heard, tasted, or smelled during your investigation.
- Include at least one image (hand-drawn or digital).
- Use three to five vocabulary words.
- Include one realistic or real quote from a fictional or real person involved.
- Include a call to action at the end. What do you want the audience to do after reading?

Eyewitness Journals

Put students in the shoes of historical figures or eyewitnesses to major events and have them write journal entries about their experiences. To deepen thinking, require students to adopt specific perspectives and points of view. For instance, after learning about the assassination of Julius Caesar, have students write from the perspective of a Roman senator, a soldier, Caesar's wife Calpurnia, or a common citizen hearing the news. This challenge helps students see how the same event could be interpreted in vastly different ways and trains them to spot bias when they read original sources.

Here are the guidelines:

- Include at least three of the five senses: what you saw, felt, heard, tasted, or smelled during your investigation.
- Use two to three vocabulary words.
- Summarize the event with a particular point of view and bias in how you describe the event and your impressions of it.

Trench Journals: A World War I Simulation

I first recognized the power of creative historical writing during a trench warfare simulation during my student teaching. My students left that day with a memorable learning experience, and they left me, for the first time, feeling like a real teacher.

Desks were split into two sides of the classroom, a "no-man's-land" running down the middle. Lights off. Black-and-white photos flickering on the screen. Machine gun fire and explosions rumbling through the speakers in the background.

As students crouched between their desk trenches, I paced through no-man's land reading excerpts from *All Quiet on the Western Front*. After each passage, students had five minutes to write a short journal entry from the perspective of a World War I soldier or nurse. What did they see? Hear? Smell? Feel? Taste? They shared their entries with a peer, and then a couple of students read theirs aloud to the class.

Some of the writing blew me away so much that I still remember it sixteen years later. Kamela wrote, "All I see are endless, dark mud walls stretching before me." And Anthony penned, "The siren rang. We knew that monstrous vapor would soon engulf our trench. I reached for my gas mask just in time. But the young private's mask across from me failed. He choked and coughed and it twisted him like a mangled puppet."

Some students who'd struggled to write a single paragraph all year turned in nearly two pages of journal entries. That lesson taught me something—all students are writers and have untapped talents waiting for the right lesson or experience to draw them out.

Glen Coleman, my high school history teacher turned mentor, stated in *Teaching in the New Crazy: On Thriving in an Overwhelming, Politicized, and Complicated World* that "a single lesson can save a life." And it can also awaken unseen talents and inspire new dreams. This is the single most beautiful thing about teaching. Despite the impossible challenges, every lesson is a chance to reach a kid, to make a difference, to change a life.

"I Am" Poems and Poetry Cafés

Bring the arts into your instruction with historical poetry. "I am" poems are a great way for students to write about historical figures or different groups. For a unit on immigration, students could write "I am" poems on Chinese, Italian, Jewish, Greek, Irish, and Japanese migrants exploring what they hoped for, feared, and faced as they began their new lives in the United States. After writing, students share their poems to find connections and differences between the groups they studied.

Want to take it further? Host a poetry café—an AVID strategy that transforms the classroom into a relaxed lounge to inspire students' inner beatnik.

Here's how to set up a poetry café:

- Turn off the fluorescents and switch on the accent lights.
- Brew some hot cocoa or tea.
- Play some jazz in the background. Keep it cool, daddy-o!
- Use finger snaps instead of applause after students read their poems.

And here are the guidelines:

- Sit in groups but write individual poems.
- Choose any form: "I am" poems (provide templates), free verse, acrostics, raps, or haikus.
- Include personal feelings, historical references, vivid imagery, and two to five vocabulary terms.
- After writing, share poems in small groups and nominate one or two peers to read to the class.

Historical Road Trip

This activity combines mapping with creative historical writing. Students take a "road trip" by visiting classroom stations that represent key events or sites from the unit. At each stop, they gather information, record journal entries, and chart their route on a map. It works beautifully for topics like the Civil Rights Movement, Westward Expansion, the Roman Empire, or the Silk Road.

It's great for teachers because once it's set up, the activity runs itself. And it's great for students because they take the wheel (or reins) for the adventure. Social history details like choosing a ride, food, and music deepen the experience and make learning feel like an adventure. (Scan the QR code for resources.)

Civil Rights Road Trip Prep

1. **CHOOSE A RIDE:** Choose an American-made automobile between the years 1955 and 1965 that cost less than $3,500.
   Year_________, Make & Model _________________ ___________________

Create a 2- minute sketch of your ride or paste an image of it here.→

GAS & COST OF TRAVEL

2. What is your car's miles per gallon? ____________
3. Average price of gas for the year of your car: ___________
4. Your road trip is 2,400 miles. How much will you spend on gas? ______

EATING ON THE ROAD

You are going to eat a lot of McDonald's on the trip. Look up a McDonald's menu from the 1950s or 1960s and decide which two items you will eat for dinner most nights and choose a drink of choice.

5. Food items & price __________________ & ___________________
6. Drink & cost______________________
7. TOTAL COST FOR DINNER _______

SOUNDTRACK TO DRIVE TO

No road trip is complete without a solid soundtrack. Choose 5 songs from 1955–1968 to rock out to when you're on the road. (But keep in mind, unless your car was made after 1966, when 8-tracks were put in some cars, you will have to hope these songs come on the radio.)

Artist	Track

Civil Rights Road Trip Map

Directions: 1. Create a map of your trip by labeling each city you stop in and a dashed line to show your travels from city to city (in order).
2. For each stop, put the date of the event.

_____/10 points

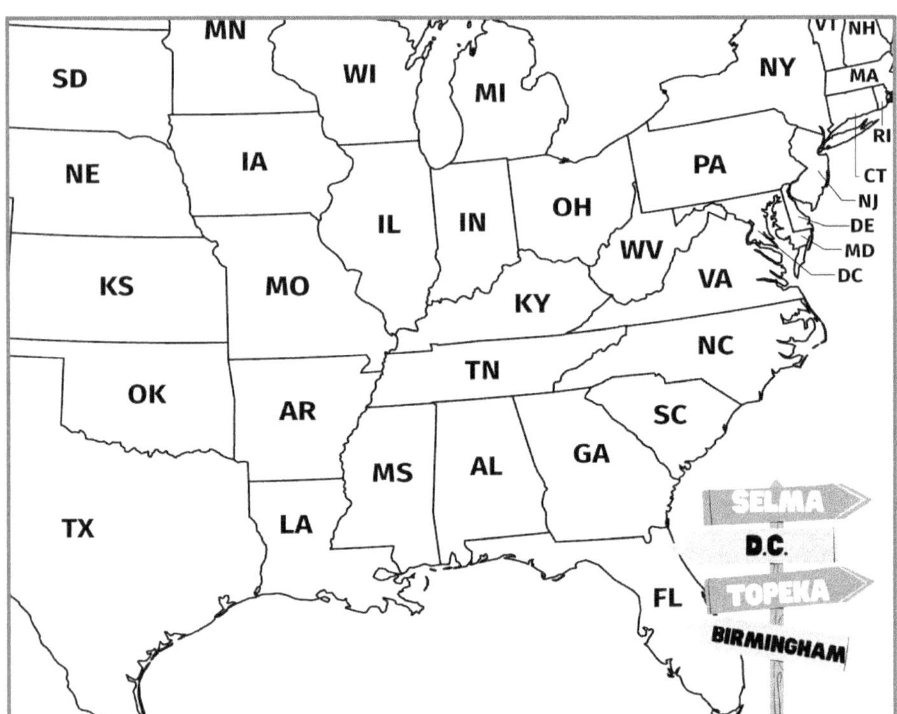

1. Which event is was farthest north? __________
2. Why did this event take place there? ____
3. Which event was farthest South? ________
4. Which event do you think was most important to create change in the US? Explain.

____

____.

Civil Rights Road Trip Journal

Directions: 1. Create short journal entries for each stop along your trip. In the boxes: Create a title for each stop that includes the city, state, and date. Below it detail what you witnessed happening there. Include **2 specific historical facts** (underline these) but also what you saw, heard, and felt as you were there! Try to make your journal entry vivid and realistic!
OPTIONAL: Instead of a journal entry– for any **two** events, you could make a sketch documenting what happened and what you experienced there. Label things if you choose.

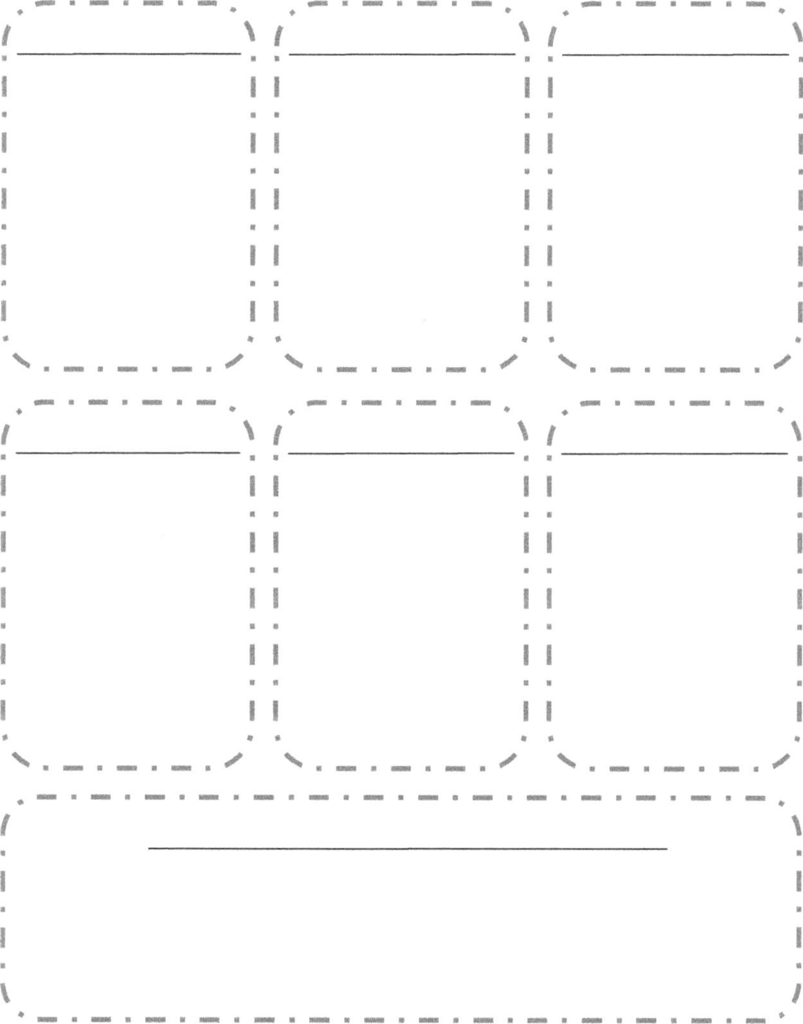

Before the activity begins, the teacher sets up the stations, turning the classroom into a series of pit stops. Each station should include images, short readings, and a hands-on artifact, if possible. A handful of spices or fake gems for the Silk Road adds a tactile hook. For a civil rights unit, I included a literacy test at the Edmund Pettus Bridge stop and two baby dolls (one white and one Black) at the *Brown v. Board of Education* site to highlight the famous doll study used in the case. These small sensory items make lasting impressions.

Here are the guidelines:

- Choose your ride. Maybe a 1955 Chevy Bel Air for a civil rights road trip or a trusty camel or yak for a Silk Road expedition.
- Plan your route. Choose a destination and chart your adventure on your map as you learn. (Teacher: Provide a few destination options.)
- Choose your meals. Use the internet for basic research to discover what people were eating at the time. A McDonald's burger and Coke or dates with goat milk?
- Choose your soundtrack. Elvis and the Beatles or traditional Chinese lute and Mongolian throat singing? (Teacher: Use their songs to create a playlist to listen to in the background as they work.)
- Hit the road. At each site, mark the location on your map and write a journal entry as if you personally visited the place or experienced the event.

Notice how much student choice is baked into this activity. Even limited choices allow students greater autonomy and ownership of their learning. In *Empower: What Happens When Students Own Their Learning*, John Spencer and A. J. Juliani encourage teachers to complete a student choice audit. Ask yourself, *What am I deciding for students that they could decide for themselves?*

This is especially important for projects.

SPARK EMPOWERMENT

Providing choice is the simplest way to increase student ownership of their learning. When students have a say in what they learn and how they show it, engagement increases and pride in workmanship follows.

Mini Projects

Projects get messy. Some students get lost and fall behind. Things rarely go exactly as planned, but that's what makes projects worthwhile. The real learning happens in the hiccups, detours, and epic fails where students need to pick up the pieces and start from scratch—hopefully having learned something more valuable than what can be measured on the rubric.

For too many years, though, I worked hard to save my students from those frustrations. I'm embarrassed to admit that I was the teacher equivalent of a helicopter parent when it came time for projects. I planned out every step, carefully guiding students through the process to make sure they stayed on track and found success in the end.

And for the most part, they did. But there was a red flag that I missed. Their projects looked remarkably similar. And that meant they were not creating; they were complying. They did not own their learning. I did.

I wanted students to be successful so badly that I didn't allow them the wonderful opportunity to face major obstacles and fail forward.

Real student-led projects leave room for risk, failure, and creative problem-solving. A group changes their topic halfway through. Another pivots to a new tool after hitting a tech roadblock. Several groups struggle to find relevant and reliable sources and need to reach out to an industry expert or librarian to get support. That's part of the process.

To prepare students for an uncertain future, we need to give them opportunities to get offtrack, stuck, and frustrated so they can learn how to fight their way through the mess. That's how they develop resilience, grit, and self-confidence. That's how they become lifelong learners ready for whatever awaits beyond the classroom.

One-Pagers

A one-pager is a creative way for students to demonstrate their learning that includes text, visuals, and design elements. Students have a single page to decorate with images, summaries, diagrams, timelines, maps, quotes, headlines, cartoons, or whatever they choose from the wide range of options provided. The more options the better. (Scan the QR code to access a one-pager template.)

These can be done digitally or on paper, but I have to admit that I'm a sucker for the handmade ones.

Here are the guidelines:

- Provide students with a single page (8½ x 11 or 11 x 17) or use Canva or Google Slides.
- Offer many choices to showcase their learning on their pages.
- Encourage originality and a central theme or style to tie everything together.

Storyboards

Storyboards are like mini graphic novels where students sequence key events with images, captions, and dialogue. They're great for gripping narratives like Cortés and the Aztec Empire, the fall of the Berlin Wall, or the election of 1800. If you're okay with "rough and ugly," they can be completed in a single class period, but for more polished and professional work, allow for more time.

Here are the guidelines:

- Use six to twelve panels, depending on time and depth.
- Use some key terms, dates, captions, and dialogue.
- Include an introduction, rising action, and a conclusion with a big takeaway.

The Deleted Scene

Want students to be more critical viewers of historical films and documentaries? Ditch the fill-in-the-blank sheet and try the deleted scene. After watching a film or documentary in class, students identify an inaccuracy, misrepresentation, or important omission. Then they rewrite the scene to fix it or add a new scene that includes a marginalized group or perspective that was missing.

Here are the guidelines:

- Choose one inaccurate or missing element from the film. (Teacher: You can identify elements for lower-level classes. Allow advanced learners to find them on their own.)
- Rewrite or add a scene with improved historical accuracy.
- You can write a script, design a storyboard, or perform a live skit.

Wonder Day Projects

A Wonder Day is a single class period devoted entirely to student curiosity. No strict directions, no detailed rubric—just a simple prompt: "Explore something you're curious about from this unit and show what you learned however you want."

The whole lesson plan could fit on a Post-it.

Though I do it a little differently, this activity was developed by John Spencer and detailed in *Empower: What Happens When Students Own Their Learning*. For Spencer, this could be a single day or extended over a full week.

Here are some guidelines and steps for a successful Wonder Day:

1. Create inquiry questions. Give students a few minutes to create a question they want to explore. For a unit on the Civil War, here are some potential questions: Were there women soldiers? How did spies impact the war? What were the best weapons being used? What did enslaved people do after emancipation?
2. Decide how to show learning. Give students a few minutes to decide how they want to show what they learn. For a single period, a Thin Slide (more on that soon), a summary, or a sketch could work. For a weeklong project, they might choose a "curiosity cast," as John Spencer calls them (a mini podcast episode), a slide show presentation, or a brief essay would work wonderfully.
3. Start exploring. Most of the lesson should be students researching and gathering evidence.
4. Wrap up. Allow a few minutes for students to share findings with peers or close with a whole-class reflection.

Test this out with a single class period. Because guess what? If it turns out to be a total mess, you only lost one day. But if you learned something about how to do it better in the future, you gained something valuable. So if you're nervous or uncertain, take that as a sign to go for it. Students need teachers who are willing to take risks and model the humility of learning from mistakes.

National History Day

For the best way to get students *doing* history—the hard, agonizing, and invigorating work of historians—there's no better practice than National History Day. It's awesome. It's intense. It might get overwhelming. And it's one of the most powerful learning experiences you can give your students.

Every year, hundreds of thousands of students around the world compete with projects that dive deep into a historical topic of their choice connected to a central theme. They dig through primary and secondary sources, craft an argument, and present their findings through essays, exhibits, websites, documentaries, or live performances. The research is real. The pressure is real. And the pride students feel when they complete their final projects? That's the real deal.

Any teacher who has done it knows the payoff is worth the stress and struggle. Once you bring your students to the district, state, and—fingers crossed—national competition and they see the results of their hard work? The feeling of accomplishment sets in. You'll fall behind on your pacing, but you'll have participated in something meaningful and hopefully unforgettable.

Presentations

At a time when AI is making it harder than ever to assess the authenticity of student work, presentations offer an invaluable way to see and hear what students have actually learned. Beyond assessment considerations, speaking clearly and confidently in front of others is a critical life skill. Whether they're in college, a boardroom, or a town hall in the future, students will need to be able to present ideas and engage an audience. Presenting is a powerful tool for both leadership and citizenship.

PechaKucha

We've all endured those painful presentations with students reading every word off their slides, backs turned to the class, voices flat like they're narrating a hostage letter at gunpoint. If that's all too familiar, try PechaKucha.

Developed in Japan, PechaKucha presentations are highly structured and ensure students know their topics and are prepared to teach them. Traditionally, they are twenty slides, with one image on each, no text, and twenty seconds per slide. It's a powerful form of visual storytelling that can work great in a history classroom. Twenty slides is a bit intense for me, so in the past, I have modified it to just five to ten.

The absence of text ensures students actually know the material. The images guide the presentation and help the presenter tell the story, while the time limit for each slide keeps the presentation moving and the audience engaged.

Here are the guidelines:

- Decide on the slide count.
- Have students research and prepare their decks.
- Allow time to rehearse and practice before presenting.

Thin Slides

Thin Slides are a rapid-fire EduProtocols presentation tool developed by Jon Corippo and Marlena Hebern that could be a great scaffold before a PechaKucha or other formal presentation. Each student creates a single slide containing one image and one word or short phrase, and these are collected in a shared slide deck for the whole class. Each student then presents their slide in twenty to forty seconds. It's fast and focused, and it helps students build confidence while teaching their peers.

Here are the guidelines:

- Assign or allow students to choose a topic.
- Allow students fifteen to twenty minutes to research and create their slide.
- Limit presentations to twenty to forty seconds per student.

Shark Tank

Want to raise the stakes? Bring in the sharks.

In *Shark Tank*–style presentations, students pitch an invention or original idea to a panel of "sharks" who ask tough questions, challenge their claims, and ultimately decide whether to invest. It works great for comparing technological advancements in ancient civilizations, for the Industrial Revolution, or even for modern reform movements.

My all-time favorite was the New Deal, but with a twist. Acting as the Brain Trust, students had to identify a problem Americans faced during the Depression that FDR's programs didn't fully address. Then they had to create their own program to solve this problem and pitch it to a congressional panel of sharks. Unlike more traditional *Shark Tank* activities, where students present a historical figure's idea or invention, this one forces them to develop, pitch, and defend their own. It's historical problem-solving with an entrepreneurial twist, and students love it.

Here are the guidelines:

- Students research an innovation or create their own.
- Presenters create a slide deck, visuals, or props and prepare their presentations.
- Sharks ask questions and decide whether to invest or approve.

You can raise the stakes and excitement further by inviting in guest sharks. I've used upperclassmen, administrators, and counselors. One year, for my online AP US History class, I brought in a student who was actually on ABC's *Shark Tank* and had secured a deal with Lori Greiner. She was the granddaughter of one of my administrators, so I scored on that one! When the stakes are raised, students almost always rise to the challenge.

Image-to-Life Skits

This is a low-stress, creative presentation that brings history to life.

Students take a historical image: a photo, painting, or cartoon—and turn it into a short skit. They can research the real story or use content knowledge and inference to dramatize what's happening. Then it's showtime. Groups come to the front, strike a pose to match the image, and when "Action!" is called, they bring it to life.

Here are the guidelines:

- Groups research the image and topic to write a short skit.
- When the image is projected, students take the stage and act it out.
- Students perform in character (with short scripts if needed), then debrief or take audience questions.

Historical Trials

Few things are as dramatic, exciting, and memorable as trials. Millennial and Gen X teachers all remember how American culture was spellbound by the O. J. Simpson trial—the Bronco chase, the bloody glove, the innocent verdict. For me, only one trial was more memorable than O.J.'s, and that was the one we enacted in Mr. Cody's sixth-grade history class.

Designed to help us understand the American justice system, the case involved a man accused of assaulting his neighbor. Though I only served on the jury, I was gripped by the drama of it all. During the weeklong trial, I took detailed notes on the lawyer's arguments and witness testimonies as I tried to determine whether my friend Todd, acting as the defendant, actually threw his neighbor down his porch steps after a heated argument or if the neighbor slipped and fell accidentally.

Though Todd was doing his best to convince me of his innocence at recess, in the lunchroom, and while playing video games after school (shameless jury tampering, no doubt), it was to no avail. When it was time for his testimony, the prosecuting attorney had him contradicting himself and poked so many holes in his story that when the jury convened, we came back with a guilty verdict. Todd was heading to the slammer for a year, and I wasn't invited over to play video games for a week.

I can't remember a single worksheet we did in that class, but I remember that trial vividly to this day. When you want the learning to stick, put history on trial.

Here are the guidelines:

- Choose a real or fictionalized historical case (Columbus, Socrates, the Rosenbergs, Joan of Arc, President Jackson).
- Assign roles: attorney, witnesses, jury, and a defendant.
- Encourage costumes, props, and getting into character.
- Don a black robe and act as the judge.

Deepening the Stakes

Projects and activities like these aren't just about creativity and variety—they're about helping students take ownership of their learning and make it meaningful by making it personal. Including a few well-timed, student-centered projects throughout the year lets students' creativity shine and gives them a deeper stake in what they're learning.

And when combined with the daily structures and strategies from earlier chapters, these projects and activities will help you build engaging and impactful units that balance fun with rigor, inquiry with skill development, and focused individual effort with collaborative learning, all while guiding students through the rich stories of history. This is how you craft a year of teaching that's energizing, purposeful, and able to spark joy in teaching and learning—day after day, unit after unit.

CONCLUSION

Ideas into Action

All that's left is the work. It's now time to put ideas into action and theory into practice.

This book has laid out a framework for making history, and your students, come alive through your teaching. You've learned how to start each class by sparking curiosity with prediction bell work—giving every student a win and getting them hooked in the first minutes of class. You've discovered routine, high-impact strategies you can weave into every unit to sharpen students' skills and confidence while keeping yourself energized for the long haul. And you've been reassured that some simple, boring lessons are okay too. Don't forget that.

You've seen how to get students doing history with primary sources and history labs—wrestling with documents, critiquing sources, and examining evidence to build the media literacy skills they need to navigate today's world. You've discovered how to lecture less but better, making direct instruction a means to entice and not just instruct. You've learned how to immerse students in the drama of the past with decision simulations, the Ken Burns classroom effect, and storytelling that brings the richness of history to the center of the curriculum. And you've learned how to get students learning from history with Harkness Discussions, Bridges to the Present activities, and historical scavenger hunts that help them see history not just as the past but as a tool to understand the present, enrich their lives, and inform their actions.

Because when students begin to find value in learning, they lean in. They get curious. They start to give a damn. And when students who have always struggled and avoided work to bypass failure begin to find success, they start trying. Compounded with our unwavering support and belief in them, that most amazing thing happens—students begin to engage and face difficulties instead of sidestepping them. And once they do, their world opens up.

I urge you to find the strategies and activities that work for you and your students and double down on those. There are no "best practices" except what helps you to teach and your students to learn. I hope you found, at the very least, a few things in this book that you are excited to put into practice. But don't let the fear of uncertainty or failure keep you from trying something new.

If we want students who are curious, confident, and willing to engage deeply in their learning, it starts with us. It starts with taking risks, experimenting, and teaching each lesson with passion and enthusiasm. Ultimately, it means embracing the challenges we face with the belief that education is, as Nelson Mandela said, "the most powerful weapon which you can use to change the world."

As teachers, we wield that weapon daily. We are the marshals of that grand army. We know there is nothing more magical than a student's eyes lighting up with the joy of discovery, nothing more powerful than a learner starting to believe in themselves. We know the transformation students can make if only they show up each day and dare to try. I hope this book has given you the confidence and the nerve to do the same.

It's up to you to be the change you want to see in the classroom.

The bell has rung. The learning awaits.

ABOUT THE AUTHOR

DAN LEWER is a teacher, author, curriculum developer, and content creator who has taught history at a Title I public school in Hawai'i for sixteen years. Named the Gilder Lehrman Institute of American History's 2020 Hawai'i History Teacher of the Year, he has collaborated with educators and schools across the country while continuing to teach in the classroom.

Through his platform History for Humans, Dan creates story-driven curriculum and videos. His online course is designed to help teachers make history more engaging, meaningful, and empowering. His work has helped thousands of teachers bring history to life in their classrooms.

Dan is available for speaking engagements and professional development workshops.

MORE FROM

DAVE BURGESS Consulting, Inc.

Since 2012, DBCI has published books that inspire and equip educators to be their best. For more information on our titles or to purchase bulk orders for your school, district, or book study, visit DaveBurgessConsulting.com/DBCIbooks.

The *Like a PIRATE*™ Series

Teach Like a PIRATE by Dave Burgess
eXPlore Like a PIRATE by Michael Matera
Learn Like a PIRATE by Paul Solarz
Plan Like a PIRATE by Dawn M. Harris
Play Like a PIRATE by Quinn Rollins
Run Like a PIRATE by Adam Welcome
Tech Like a PIRATE by Matt Miller

The *Lead Like a PIRATE*™ Series

Lead Like a PIRATE by Shelley Burgess and Beth Houf
Balance Like a PIRATE by Jessica Cabeen, Jessica Johnson, and Sarah Johnson
Lead beyond Your Title by Nili Bartley
Lead with Appreciation by Amber Teamann and Melinda Miller
Lead with Collaboration by Allyson Apsey and Jessica Gomez
Lead with Culture by Jay Billy
Lead with Instructional Rounds by Vicki Wilson

Lead with Literacy by Mandy Ellis
She Leads by Dr. Rachael George and Majalise W. Tolan

The EduProtocol Field Guide Series

Deploying EduProtocols by Kim Voge, with Jon Corippo and Marlena Hebern
Designing EduProtocols by Mark Wallace, with Jon Corippo and Marlena Hebern
The EduProtocol Field Guide by Marlena Hebern and Jon Corippo
The EduProtocol Field Guide AI Literacy Edition by Kate Meyer and Nicole Davis, with Jon Corippo and Marlena Hebern
The EduProtocol Field Guide Book 2 by Marlena Hebern and Jon Corippo
The EduProtocol Field Guide ELA Edition by Jacob Carr
The EduProtocol Field Guide Math Edition by Lisa Nowakowski and Jeremiah Ruesch
The EduProtocol Field Guide Primary Edition by Benjamin Cogswell and Jennifer Dean
The EduProtocol Field Guide Social Studies Edition by Dr. Scott M. Petri and Adam Moler

Leadership & School Culture

Autopilot by Rich Czyz
Be 1% Better by Ron Clark
Be THAT Teacher by Dwayne Reed
Beyond the Surface of Restorative Practices by Marisol Rerucha
Change the Narrative by Henry J. Turner and Kathy Lopes
Choosing to See by Pamela Seda and Kyndall Brown
Culturize by Jimmy Casas
Discipline Win by Andy Jacks
Educate Me! by Dr. Shree Walker with Michael D. Ison

Escaping the School Leader's Dunk Tank by Rebecca Coda and Rick Jetter
Fight Song by Kim Bearden
From Teacher to Leader by Starr Sackstein
If the Dance Floor Is Empty, Change the Song by Joe Clark
The Innovator's Mindset by George Couros
It's OK to Say "They" by Christy Whittlesey
Kids Deserve It! by Todd Nesloney and Adam Welcome
Leading the Whole Teacher by Allyson Apsey
Let Them Speak by Rebecca Coda and Rick Jetter
The Limitless School by Abe Hege and Adam Dovico
Live Your Excellence by Jimmy Casas
Next-Level Teaching by Jonathan Alsheimer
The Pepper Effect by Sean Gaillard
Principaled by Kate Barker, Kourtney Ferrua, and Rachael George
The Principled Principal by Jeffrey Zoul and Anthony McConnell
Relentless by Hamish Brewer
The Secret Solution by Todd Whitaker, Sam Miller, and Ryan Donlan
Start. Right. Now. by Todd Whitaker, Jeffrey Zoul, and Jimmy Casas
Stop. Right. Now. by Jimmy Casas and Jeffrey Zoul
Teach Your Class Off by CJ Reynolds
Teachers Deserve It by Rae Hughart and Adam Welcome
They Call Me "Mr. De" by Frank DeAngelis
Thrive through the Five by Jill M. Siler
Unmapped Potential by Julie Hasson and Missy Lennard
When Kids Lead by Todd Nesloney and Adam Dovico
Word Shift by Joy Kirr
Your School Rocks by Ryan McLane and Eric Lowe

Technology & Tools

50 Ways to Engage Students with Google Apps by Alice Keeler and Heather Lyon

50 Things to Go Further with Google Classroom by Alice Keeler and Libbi Miller

50 Things You Can Do with Google Classroom by Alice Keeler and Libbi Miller

140 Twitter Tips for Educators by Brad Currie, Billy Krakower, and Scott Rocco

AI Optimism by Becky Keene

Block Breaker by Brian Aspinall

Building Blocks for Tiny Techies by Jamila "Mia" Leonard

Code Breaker by Brian Aspinall

The Complete EdTech Coach by Katherine Goyette and Adam Juarez

Control Alt Achieve by Eric Curts

The Esports Education Playbook by Chris Aviles, Steve Isaacs, Christine Lion-Bailey, and Jesse Lubinsky

Google Apps for Littles by Christine Pinto and Alice Keeler

Master the Media by Julie Smith

Raising Digital Leaders by Jennifer Casa-Todd

Reality Bytes by Christine Lion-Bailey, Jesse Lubinsky, and Micah Shippee, PhD

Sail the 7 Cs with Microsoft Education by Becky Keene and Kathi Kersznowski

Shake Up Learning by Kasey Bell

Social LEADia by Jennifer Casa-Todd

Stepping Up to Google Classroom by Alice Keeler and Kimberly Mattina

Teaching Math with Google Apps by Alice Keeler and Diana Herrington

Teaching with Google Jamboard by Alice Keeler and Kimberly Mattina
Teachingland by Amanda Fox and Mary Ellen Weeks

Teaching Methods & Materials

All 4s and 5s by Andrew Sharos
Boredom Busters by Katie Powell
Building Strong Writers by Christina Schneider
The Classroom Chef by John Stevens and Matt Vaudrey
The Collaborative Classroom by Trevor Muir
Copyrighteous by Diana Gill
CREATE by Bethany J. Petty
Ditch That Homework by Matt Miller and Alice Keeler
Ditch That Textbook by Matt Miller
Don't Ditch That Tech by Matt Miller, Nate Ridgway, and Angelia Ridgway
EDrenaline Rush by John Meehan
Educated by Design by Michael Cohen, The Tech Rabbi
Empowered to Choose: A Practical Guide to Personalized Learning by Andrew Easton
Expedition Science by Becky Schnekser
Frustration Busters by Katie Powell
Fully Engaged by Michael Matera and John Meehan
Game On? Brain On! by Lindsay Portnoy, PhD
Guided Math AMPED by Reagan Tunstall
Happy & Resilient by Roni Habib
Innovating Play by Jessica LaBar-Twomy and Christine Pinto
Instant Relevance by Denis Sheeran
Instructional Coaching Connection by Nathan Lang-Raad
Keeping the Wonder by Jenna Copper, Ashley Bible, Abby Gross, and Staci Lamb
LAUNCH by John Spencer and A.J. Juliani
Learning in the Zone by Dr. Sonny Magana

Less Talk, More Action by Allyson Apsey and Emily Freeland
Lights, Cameras, TEACH! by Kevin J. Butler
The Magical CTE Classroom by Tisha Richmond
Make Learning MAGICAL by Tisha Richmond
Pass the Baton by Kathryn Finch and Theresa Hoover
Playing with Purpose by Michael Matera and John Meehan
Project-Based Learning Anywhere by Lori Elliott
Pure Genius by Don Wettrick
The Revolution by Darren Ellwein and Derek McCoy
The Science Box by Kim Adsit and Adam Peterson
Shift This! by Joy Kirr
Skyrocket Your Teacher Coaching by Michael Cary Sonbert
Spark Learning by Ramsey Musallam
Sparks in the Dark by Travis Crowder and Todd Nesloney
Table Talk Math by John Stevens
Teachables by Cheryl Abla and Lisa Maxfield
Unpack Your Impact by Naomi O'Brien and LaNesha Tabb
The Wild Card by Hope and Wade King
Writefully Empowered by Jacob Chastain
The Writing on the Classroom Wall by Steve Wyborney
You Are Poetry by Mike Johnston
You'll Never Guess What I'm Saying by Naomi O'Brien
You'll Never Guess What I'm Thinking About by Naomi O'Brien

Inspiration, Professional Growth & Personal Development

Becoming the BISON by Kim Gameroz
Be REAL by Tara Martin
Be the One for Kids by Ryan Sheehy
The Coach ADVenture by Amy Illingworth
Creatively Productive by Lisa Johnson
The Ed Branding Book by Dr. Renae Bryant and Lynette White
Educational Eye Exam by Alicia Ray
The EduNinja Mindset by Jennifer Burdis

Empower Our Girls by Lynmara Colón and Adam Welcome
Finding Lifelines by Andrew Grieve and Andrew Sharos
The Four O'Clock Faculty by Rich Czyz
How Much Water Do We Have? by Pete and Kris Nunweiler
P Is for Pirate by Dave and Shelley Burgess
A Passion for Kindness by Tamara Letter
The Path to Serendipity by Allyson Apsey
PheMOMenal Teacher by Annick Rauch
Recipes for Resilience by Robert A. Martinez
Rogue Leader by Rich Czyz
Sanctuaries by Dan Tricarico
Saving Sycamore by Molly B. Hudgens
The Secret Sauce by Rich Czyz
Shattering the Perfect Teacher Myth by Aaron Hogan
Stories from Webb by Todd Nesloney
Talk to Me by Kim Bearden
Teach Better by Chad Ostrowski, Tiffany Ott, Rae Hughart, and Jeff Gargas
Teacher by Day by Dr. Yvette Dixon Ledford
Teach Me, Teacher by Jacob Chastain
Teach, Play, Learn! by Adam Peterson
The Teachers of Oz by Herbie Raad and Nathan Lang-Raad
Teaching Is a Tattoo by Mike Johnston
Teaching the Ms. Abbott Way by Joyce Stephens Abbott
TeamMakers by Laura Robb and Evan Robb
Through the Lens of Serendipity by Allyson Apsey
Write Here and Now by Dan Tricarico
The Zen Teacher by Dan Tricarico

Children's Books

Alpert by LaNesha Tabb
Alpert Becomes an Author by LaNesha Tabb
Alpert Finds a Problem by LaNesha Tabb

Alpert & Friends by LaNesha Tabb
Beyond Us by Aaron Polansky
Cannonball In by Tara Martin
Dolphins in Trees by Aaron Polansky
Dragon Smart by Tisha and Tommy Richmond
I Can Achieve Anything by MoNique Waters
I Want to Be a Lot by Ashley Savage
The Magic of Wonder by Jenna Copper, Ashley Bible, Abby Gross, and Staci Lamb
Micah's Big Question by Naomi O'Brien
The Princes of Serendip by Allyson Apsey
Ride with Emilio by Richard Nares
A Teacher's Top Secret Confidential by LaNesha Tabb
A Teacher's Top Secret: Mission Accomplished by LaNesha Tabb
The Wild Card Kids by Hope and Wade King
Zom-Be a Design Thinker by Amanda Fox

www.ingramcontent.com/pod-product-compliance
Lightning Source LLC
LaVergne TN
LVHW010700110826
845149LV00014B/3183

* 9 7 8 1 9 6 8 8 9 8 2 3 6 *